DIGITAL IMAGE EDITING & SPECIAL EFFECTS

DIGITAL IMAGE EDITING & SPECIAL EFFECTS

MASTER THE KEY TECHNIQUES OF PHOTOSHOP & LIGHTROOM

Michael Freeman

ILEX

First published in the UK in 2013 by:

I L E X

210 High Street
Lewes
East Sussex
BN7 2NS
www.ilex-press.com

Distributed worldwide (except North America) by
Thames & Hudson Ltd., 181A High Holborn, London
WC1V 7QX, United Kingdom

Publisher: Alastair Campbell
Associate Publisher: Adam Juniper
Managing Editor: Natalia Price-Cabrera
Editor: Tara Gallagher
Specialist Editor: Frank Gallaugher
Creative Director: James Hollywell
Senior Designer: Ginny Zeal
Designer: Richard Wolfströme
Colour Origination: Ivy Press Reprographics

British Library Cataloguing-in-Publication Data
A catalogue record for this book is available from
the British Library.

ISBN: 978-1-78157-995-4

Printed and bound in China

10 9 8 7 6 5 4 3 2 1

CONTENTS

1

SOFTWARE TOOLS & TECHNIQUES

2
IMAGE ENHANCEMENT

3
IMAGE RETOUCHING

4
SPECIAL EFFECTS

Introduction

Digital photography not only brings processing in-house and onto your desktop, it actually extends photography. By this, I mean that shooting can be treated as just the starting point in the creation of an image. The latest versions of processing and image-editing software, including Photoshop, Lightroom, Aperture, and several others, have sophisticated tools for doing two things: one is extracting the maximum possible visual information from a Raw file, the other is interpreting the image in as many ways as possible to suit the user's individual taste.

Even though you might be doing both at the same time when you process, in concept and purpose they are quite different functions. For photographers who are mainly interested in shooting, and who reject the idea of any kind of manipulation, the main job of an image-editing program is to get the best tonal and color result from the Raw file. It goes without saying that serious photography needs the data that is preserved when you shoot Raw, the only sensible exception being news and sports photography that needs to be delivered and run instantly. This is where this book begins, and the possibilities for treating a single image now exceed by far what was once the domain of the darkroom expert.

But photography can be taken into different areas, far away from the straight shot. There is, for instance, the panorama made of stitched overlapping images. And HDR, in which a sequence of different exposures is combined to cover a much greater dynamic range than the camera's sensor can capture. Colors and tones can be altered to extremes, images can be montaged, and text added. Depending on your interests and needs, the computer and appropriate software can be a workshop for manipulating and using the images you shot.

Michael Freeman

1

Software Tools & Techniques

Software packages

Like digital cameras, image-editing software has come a long way in a relatively short space of time. Of course, individual programs vary in price and complexity, but the average image-editor is now rich in features and capable of making amendments and enhancements to photographs in a way that was undreamt of five years ago.

Perhaps the greatest change in more recent times has been the emergence of Raw editors, such as Adobe Lightroom and Apple Aperture, as "one-stop" shops for image processing. As we shall see, such programs now offer extensive (and localized) image-editing capabilities that often negate the need for further post-production work in what are often referred to as "pixel editors," such as Photoshop and PaintShop Pro. Raw editors now offer many professionals

(and amateurs) a fast and efficient processing workflow and cataloging option in one easy-to-use package. If you're not into or don't need image manipulation down to the pixel level, then a Raw editor may be all you need.

However, there are many photographers who, for one reason or another, need to be able to manipulate their images at a more localized level than is possible with a Raw editor, and there are still a great many image-editing program options available to them.

The industry-leading software and the one used by the majority of professionals is Adobe's Photoshop. Photoshop offers unrivalled image-editing tools, and as it is the one program that most others aim to emulate it's the software used throughout this title. The tools vary

somewhat between programs, but using Photoshop tool icons, names, and commands will reach the broadest possible audience.

The high price of Photoshop, however, puts it out of the reach of most non-professional users, who instead opt for one of a number of mid-level programs, such as Photoshop Elements, Corel PaintShop Pro, Roxio Creator, or Serif Digital Photo Suite.

Although these programs don't offer the same level of sophistication (or share the same steep learning curve) as Photoshop, they fulfil most photographers' requirements at a fraction of the price, and most have the tools to perform the vast majority of techniques and projects in this book, if only in a slightly different way and with slightly different tools.

↑ Adobe's flagship image-editing program, Photoshop, has been described as "an industry standard for graphics professionals." And it's worth noting that Photoshop also features ACR (Adobe Camera Raw), which offers almost the same Raw processing tools that are available in Adobe Lightroom, as they share the same software engine.

↑ Adobe's Photoshop Elements is probably the best-selling, mid-range image-editing suite. Compatible with both Mac and PC it has a very rich editing toolset, provides intuitive ways to make slideshows and other viewing projects, enables geotagging, and a whole host of other features.

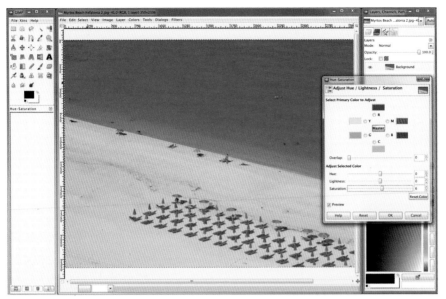

← GIMP (GNU Image Manipulation Program) is a free image-editing program available on both Mac and Windows operating systems. It offers numerous powerful image-editing tools, and is often compared with Photoshop in terms of its structure and editing capabilities. As a free, open-source program, it's certainly worth experimenting with if you want to get a taste of more advanced image-editing software.

← Adobe Photoshop Lightroom has been developed to help serious amateur and pro photographers keep track of their images, while also allowing for rapid editing tasks, such as color saturation, grayscale conversion, exposure, and so on. The focus is more on batch processing, general image optimization, and cataloging and viewing rather than intensive, localized image-editing work; however, features such as the Adjustment Brush and the Graduated Filter do allow for a surprising degree of local adjustment.

The toolbox

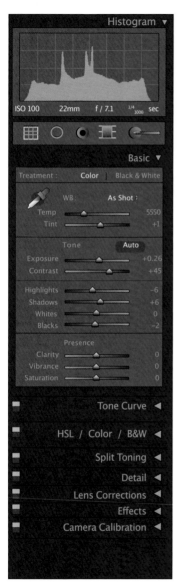

Lightroom

Every image-editing program has a toolbox, a clearly defined area where you can find the various tools you'll need to correct, amend, or enhance an image. The toolbox for each program will vary, but typical tools include brushes, selection tools, text tools, erasers, cropping tools, and so on. When you click on a particular tool icon in the toolbox, the cursor will change to the appropriate icon, indicating you have selected that particular tool.

The toolbox is the most used part of the editing program's interface. It should be easy to locate, but discreet so as not to interfere with your work. Learning what the various tools do is, naturally enough, a fundamental aspect of image editing, although how you do this is up to you. Most of the more popular programs have various "wizards" that will either take you through specific tasks, or at least tell you the name of a tool if you leave the cursor over the icon for a set amount of time.

There is certainly a learning curve when familiarizing yourself with image-editing software, but hopefully one that you'll find enjoyable and rewarding, although undoubtedly there will be some frustrating moments along the way. Remember you can always go back a step if you click the wrong button. Discovering how to do this should be a priority; more often than not Ctrl/⌘ + Z will work.

With many applications, not all the tools are constantly on display. As you continue to learn the program, you'll notice that tools that perform a similar task are often grouped together, such as the selection tools, the drawing tools, and the eraser tools, for example. This not only helps you when navigating the toolbox, but—depending on the specific program—you may find that only one of a particular group is displayed at any one time, and that to select an alternative but closely associated tool, you'll need to activate a pull-down menu by clicking in a certain part of the tool icon.

Along with the basic toolbox, many mid-range programs also have tool option bars and menus, which allow you to adjust the functionality of certain tools, such as the way they interact with the image, or their shape and size. Learning the tool options is as important as learning the tools themselves.

Other controls are found in panels or panes that can be opened and closed as and when needed, and in dialog boxes that appear whenever a particular operation offers detailed choices. In most editing suites, many of the tools and controls can be selected using the keyboard; you'll find, as you become increasingly familiar with the software, that this is the most efficient way to work.

Photoshop Elements 10

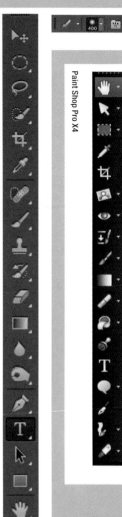

Photoshop CS6

Paint Shop Pro X4

GIMP

Icons

There is a crossover of icons between many of the more popular image-editing programs, as shown here between Photoshop, Photoshop Elements, and Paint Shop Pro. GIMP's tool icons are also similar in many cases, but some provide a more meaningful description.

Histograms

The histogram lies at the heart of all digital images. Although they may at first seem daunting, they are, in fact, quite easy to understand, and it only takes a relatively short amount of time to grasp their significance. Learn to read histograms—either on your camera's LCD screen or in an image-editing program—and you're well on the way to being able to assess a digital image. The examples here show you what to look for.

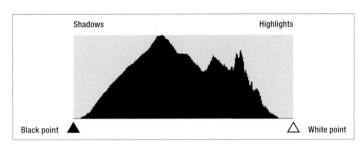

Shadows · Highlights

Black point ▲ · △ White point

↑ A histogram is a way of showing the tonal distribution of an image in the form of a graph. The left side of the histogram represents dark tones, with black being the furthest left-hand point. The central portion represents the midtones, and the right side represents the light tones, with white being the furthest right-hand point. The shape of the histogram is determined by the number of pixels for any given tone. A dark image, for example, will have most pixels arranged on the left side. When reviewing histograms check that pixels aren't bunched against the left- or right-hand side, as this indicates pixels are either pure black or pure white and contain no detail.

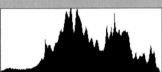

Skyline
This city view with billowing clouds divides into three main tonal groups in the histogram: the largest group is the blue sky and darker buildings, to the right is the pale gray parts of the clouds, and the small area at far right is the white cloud.

Statue
More than a third of the image is in deep shadow—the tones at far left crowding the edge, showing loss of detail—while the toes and two people carry a range of tones stretching in steps to the right. The small line at far right is the highlights on the white cloth.

Deer

This histogram is not dissimilar to that of the Indian worshippers opposite—deep shadows with the curve falling sharply away to the right. However, even more of the image is dark here, and while the highlights—the small blip at right—are important to the image, the main subject, the deer, is itself dark.

Cocktails

The message from this histogram is that this shot contains several tonal groups, but evenly spread from shadow to highlight. The histogram has no major bias, but a number of smaller peaks.

Priest

Three components of the histogram reflect the three obvious tonal groups in the picture: dark surrounding shadow gives the sharp peak to the left, the dark bridge is the "plateau" to the right, while the white-robed Japanese priest is represented by the tiny group of spikes at the far right.

Using Levels

The Levels command is central to most image-editing programs. It is a powerful yet intuitive way to adjust an image's overall brightness and contrast. In addition, as we shall see here, Levels can also be used to correct a color cast. The Levels dialog box contains a histogram of the image, and in most cases, when you first open a photograph on the screen, at least when shooting JPEGs or TIFFs, one of the first things you're likely to do is to go to Levels (*Image > Adjustments > Levels*) and check the picture's tonal distribution.

Is it too dark or too bright? Is there an even distribution of pixels across the histogram? Does the image look flat and washed out? It's possible to address all these issues quickly using Levels.

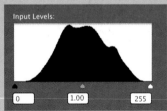

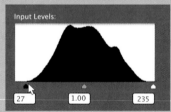

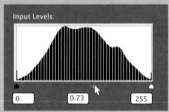

↑ This image of rose-colored rock looks washed out and lacking in contrast. Opening the Levels command in Photoshop (Ctrl/⌘ + L) to review the histogram shows that although there is an even distribution of tones, there are no black or white pixels. There is a gap between both the black point and the start of the histogram on the left, and the white point and the start of the histogram on the right.

↑ In order to "optimize" the image so that contrast is at its fullest extent, the white point slider is moved left to sit under the right end of the histogram, and the black point slider is moved right so that it sits under the left end of the histogram. The image now exhibits much stronger contrast, and the colors also appear richer.

↑ Here the gray point (or gamma) slider has been moved to the right (effectively making a greater number of pixels fall into the left side—shadow region—of the histogram). As you might expect the image has become even darker. Moving the gray point to the left would effectively make the image lighter.

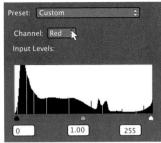

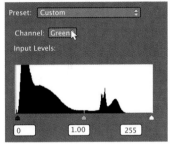

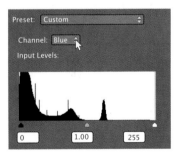

↑ This photograph was taken in late afternoon, and the warm light of the approaching sunset has given the image an overall pinkish color cast. More often than not, it's acceptable to leave this type of color cast uncorrected, as it brings a pleasing warm glow to an image, but here it's just too strong. You can use Levels to correct color issues as well as contrast and brightness. With the Levels dialog box open, it's possible to select one of the three primary colors (or channels) that make up all digital photographs: red, green, and blue. (See Channels & Layers, page 20). Selecting the red channel shows that, not surprisingly, there is a good spread of red throughout the image. But selecting first the green and then the blue channel shows these colors are severely lacking in the highlight region of the image. By moving the white point slider so that it sits under the histogram in both the green and blue channels results in a much more accurately colored image.

As we've seen, the Levels command is a very effective way of adjusting the overall brightness and contrast of an image, as well as providing you with a way of adjusting the tonal values of a specific color channel. However, some editing suites, such as Photoshop, Elements, and Paint Shop Pro, provide an even more powerful way of making contrast and color adjustments.

Known simply as "Curves," the Curves tool allows you to make much more localized adjustments to any part of your image. This makes the Curves tool far more flexible than Levels, and although it takes a little longer to learn, it's the adjustment method of choice for most professional photographers. You can access Curves via *Image > Adjustments > Curves* or use Ctrl/⌘ + M.

← This shot of a white, timber-clad house is very contrasting. In order to ensure that the house didn't over-expose, an exposure had to be set that resulted in an underexposed foreground. The Curves command consists of a diagonal line, which represents the tonal range of the image. Like Levels, the linear curve line has a black point (bottom left) and a white point (top right). Clicking with the cursor (eyedropper) on a very dark element of the image will result in the relevant area being highlighted on the linear curve —indicated by a small circle.

← To lighten this area, simply click on the line where the circle was, and drag the line upward slightly. You'll notice the entire image becomes brighter. We can address that at the next stage. At this point, we simply want to ensure that the shadow regions have a little more detail in them.

← Having fixed the dark foreground, it's time to bring the bright highlights down. Clicking on the brightest part of the image with the eyedropper shows these to be near the top right of the curve. Click on the curve and drag it down to darken the highlights. You'll see that the shadow point remains where it was and you now have an inverted S-shaped curve, which by lightening shadows and darkening highlights has reduced contrast.

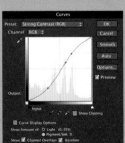

↑ To make life quicker and easier when using Curves, more recent versions of Photoshop and Photoshop Elements have a number of preset linear curve adjustments available in the Preset pull-down menu.

These will automatically create curves that lighten, darken, cross-process, turn an image into its negative, or increase contrast, either marginally or by quite a substantial amount as shown here. You can use these settings and then click

other points on the line to fine-tune the adjustment.

As with Levels, it's possible to edit each color channel individually for a really accurate way to fix any color cast your image may have.

All color images from a digital camera are made up of the three primary colors—red, green, and blue. These respective color components can be viewed as the red, green, and blue channel. As well as these three channels, any new selection or Path that you create can be saved as a new channel, known as an alpha channel. These are covered later in the book. Channels can be switched on and off individually, both to view and to edit, as we've just seen with the Levels and Curves commands.

Understanding Channels will also help you when you want to convert a color image into a grayscale one.

Layers are a fundamental aspect of most image-editing applications, and are used widely in just about every image-editing task. Adding new layers allows you to alter or add new elements to an image so that the overall appearance is affected, but without impacting on the original or "Background" layer—this is known as "non-destructive editing."

Layers can be used in a variety of ways, either to make a whole range of adjustments to a single image, or to put a number of separate images together to make one composite.

Later in the book, we'll be covering projects that utilize layers, but for now it's useful to simply familiarize yourself with the concept of layers and how you can view and arrange them.

RGB

Red channel

Green channel

↑ A color image from a digital camera contains three channels: red, green, and blue. Each of these channels can be edited individually—via the Channels palette—as one may exhibit more image artifacts such as noise. Working on the worst-offending channel makes it easier to make corrections, with less potentially degrading interference to the rest of the image.

Blue channel

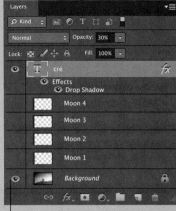

Visibility eye

Blending modes | Opacity setting

↑ Photoshop's Layers panel displays the various layers used to make up the final image, stacked one on top of the other. In the example shown here, the Background layer contains the image of the tree. A photograph of the moon was then copied and pasted over the Background layer and duplicated three times, creating the moon layers as shown in the top Layers panel. Clicking on each of the Moon layers in turn enabled the duplicate moons to be resized and repositioned. The text layer sits above these layers, and to make it stand out, a Drop Shadow effect layer was added.

Layers are incredibly flexible. You can change their order so that, for example, some changes apply only to certain elements of an image. You can make a layer visible or invisible by clicking on the Visibility Eye. In the second image, all the moon layers have been "switched off," leaving just the Background and text layers. It's also possible to reduce the opacity of any given layer using the Opacity slider. Finally, you have an option of various blending modes, which determine how one layer interacts with another (see page 26). Many of these features will be used in projects later in the book, when their functions and how to use them will be covered more fully. It's usual practice to "flatten" the image (*Layer > Flatten Image*) when you're happy. This puts all the components onto one layer, keeping the file size down.

Adjustment layers

Now that you have a basic grasp of Layers—what they are, and how they work—it's time to look at a group of layers that were designed specifically with the photographer in mind—adjustment layers.

Adjustment layers are similar to normal layers, but differ in that rather than adding or changing pixel information, adjustment layers can be thought of as a set of instructions that alter the overall look of an image. Adjustment layers, therefore, are a convenient and efficient way of making standard image adjustments, such as Levels or Hue/Saturation commands, in a non-destructive way, that is without affecting the original background image. The real beauty of adjustment layers is that you can return to an adjustment layer you created earlier any time during the editing stage and adjust the values and therefore the look of the image should you wish to do so. In fact, you can keep making adjustments to improve the image right up to the point where you flatten the image for printing or publishing on the web.

← This image of a group of sailboat masts has some graphic potential but appears very flat.

↓ Going to *Layer > New Adjustment Layer > Levels...* brings up a Levels command. The large gaps between either side of the histogram and the black-and-white points shows just how lacking in contrast the image is. Simply dragging both black-and-white points so they sit underneath the histogram optimizes the image to give it a complete tonal range from pure black to pure white. The result is an instant boost to the image.

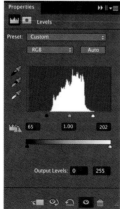

↓ Although the image looks much stronger, we can make the sky even bluer by creating a Hue/Saturation adjustment layer (*Layer > New Adjustment Layer > Hue/Saturation...*). In the Hue/Saturation dialog box, Blues have been selected in the pull-down menu and the Saturation slider moved a long way to the right to increase the color of the sky. Return to the Layers palette and you'll see both the Levels and Hue/Saturation adjustment layers are visible.

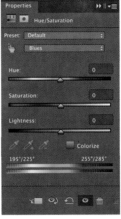

↓ In this final adjustment, a black-and-white adjustment layer was created to experiment with the white masts and cloud sitting above a near black sky. The strength of adjustment layers lies in the fact that you can keep returning to your changes by clicking on the black-and-white circle (layer thumbnail) icon in the relevant adjustment layer's layer. Another advantage is the presence of an active layer mask, which can be accessed by clicking on the small square (thumbnail) in the adjustment layer. Layer masks is the next subject we will tackle.

It may be that some, or even all, of the adjustments you want to make to an image ideally should be applied only to certain areas of the photo. Layer masks allow you to do this.

The term "mask" has passed on from traditional, film reprographics, in which part of the image was physically masked off using a sheet of red plastic (commonly the brand Rubylith), which was painstakingly cut to fit over the area that was to be masked off. As a result of this, the masked area does not undergo any changes being made to the rest of the image.

Applying digital masks is much easier, doesn't involve the use of sharp knives, and with care will result in a more accurate mask. In Elements, layer masks are restricted only to adjustment layers, but in Photoshop they can be applied to any layer. They work by painting black or white to either hide or reveal, for example, a special-effects filter layer; and it's possible to quickly switch between the two to add to or subtract from an existing mask to alter the effect it has on the image.

← Here we're going to use a Layer Mask to create a freeze zoom special effect. The Background image of the Buddhist temple was duplicated (*Layer > Duplicate Layer...*), and using the Radial Blur filter (*Filter > Blur > Radial Blur*) a zoom blur was applied.

↓ In the Layers panel, with the Zoom layer selected, clicking on the "Add layer mask" icon creates a Layer Mask for that specific layer. The mask takes the form of a blank white square. The outline around the square indicates that the mask is active.

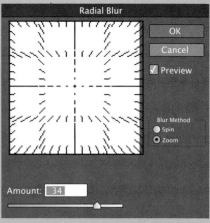

↑ Now with the Layer Mask active we're going to mask off the Buddha statue from the zoom effect, so that it isn't blurred. First, ensure that the foreground color is set to black at the bottom of the Toolbox (simply press "D" for default and then "X" to swap white and black) and using an appropriately sized brush (use the "[" and "]" keys to alter the brush size) paint over the statue. With each brush stroke, the layer beneath will be made more visible. Returning to the Layers palette we can see the mask being produced; it appears as black. You can amend the mask simply by painting with white (press "X") to bring the zoom effect back.

Blending modes

As mentioned in the discussion on Layers, Photoshop offers a staggering number of ways in which layers can interact with one another.

Blending modes work by assessing the color and/or brightness values of the pixels on one layer, and then altering the values of pixels on the layer above depending on the specific blending mode. Blending modes can be used successfully in combination with layer masks and adjustment layers.

There are over 20 individual blending modes in Photoshop, but for photography you're unlikely to use many of them— their purpose really lies in graphics and illustration. However, one or two have something to offer photographers, primarily in controlling exposure, and we'll look at these here. Other modes will be used in projects later in the book. It's worth experimenting with a couple of images, or even a duplicate image to get a feel for what the various modes do. With the Move tool selected, you can scroll down and apply each mode by holding down the Shift key and pressing "+" (plus) or "-" (minus).

↓ Because of the bright light, powerful fill-in flash, and light colors in this shot, it looks a little overexposed. This could be addressed using a Levels or Curves adjustment layer, but an alternative way to tackle overexposure is to duplicate the background layer (simply drag it to the New Layer icon, second from the right at the bottom of the panel) and select Multiply from the blending mode pull-down menu. Afterward you can fine-tune the strength of the effect using the Opacity slider.

← Due to the backlit nature of this shot, the foreground and the buildings in the background are underexposed.

→ Duplicating the background and using the Screen blending mode will effectively increase the exposure.

← The foreground and buildings are now brighter, but because the blending mode was applied to the entire image, the sky is now overexposed.

→ To fix this add a Layer Mask to the Screen layer by clicking on the "Add layer mask" icon in the Layers palette.

↑ With the foreground color set to black at the bottom of the Toolbox (press D and then X), and with the Screen Layer Mask active, use a large soft brush to erase the Screen effect.

↑ The final image is much more evenly balanced in terms of exposure. The same result can be achieved in Elements using any adjustment layer—with the blending mode set to Screen—as they automatically come with a Layer Mask.

Selection tools

Using Layer Masks is one way to restrict changes to a specific area of an image, but as with most image-editing tasks, there are other ways in which you can isolate specific areas or objects. Most image-editing applications have a number of selection tools. These can be used to select a general area, in order to increase the brightness in a specific region, for example, or they can be utilized to precisely cut out an object.

The more sophisticated the image-editing program, the greater the number of selection options you'll have. This is because not all selections are of a similar type—choosing all the areas of the same color, for example, is very different to making a cutout of a subject comprising a variety of different colors. In other words certain subjects are better suited to one type of selection than another. In addition some people prefer

one method of selection over another; while it's often the case that a combination of selection routines provides the best final result.

Over the next few pages we'll take a look at the various selection tools commonly used in Photoshop, and the methods associated with them. The vast majority of these are also available in Elements and other mid-range editing programs.

Modify buttons

You can add to and subtract from selections using the keyboard together with the selection tool.

To add to an existing selection hold down the Shift key as you start to draw. You'll notice a small "+" symbol appears next to the cursor.

To subtract part of the selection hold down the Alt/⌘ key. A small "–" symbol will appear next to the cursor.

← In this example, a circular marquee was drawn around the beach ball; the Shift key was used to create a perfect circle. The selection was inverted (*Select > Inverse*) to select the water and not the ball. Using the Hue/Saturation dialog box (*Image > Adjustments > Hue/Saturation*) the color of the water was changed.

Marquee tools

The Marquee tools create a regular-shaped selection, visible as a dotted line (often referred to as "marching ants"). There are four Marquee tools: Rectangular, Elliptical, Single Row, and Single Column. To draw a marquee, simply click and drag the cursor to form a box or ellipse over the area you want to select. To move the marquee, place the cursor inside the marquee's borders, click, and drag it with the mouse. Holding down the Shift key will create a perfect square or circular shape. Although this is one of the fastest selection methods, it has little practical use in photography due to the regularity of the shapes available. However, the Marquee tools can be useful in creating borders, or when used in conjunction with a heavily feathered edge to create a vignette. As with other selection tools, the selection can be modified using the Refine Edge dialog (see page 32).

Lasso tools

The Lasso tools, like the Marquee tools, allow you to define a shape as the selection, but are much more flexible. There are three Lasso tools: the Freehand Lasso, the Polygonal Lasso, and the Magnetic Lasso. With the freehand Lasso tool selected you can draw around any shape as long as you hold down the mouse; the selection being completed when you join the line to its start point. Release the mouse at any point and the selection will be completed with a straight line directly to the start point. The Polygonal Lasso tool allows you to draw any shape, but with straight lines. Click to start, drag the mouse along a line, and click again to make the selection. Repeat until you have completed the selection by returning to the start point. The Magnetic Lasso tool is a more powerful option. It's capable of tracing an outline as long as there is sufficient contrast between the subject and the background. Place the cursor at the beginning of the selection and move the cursor along the outline of the shape you're selected. You'll see the line of marching ants "cling" to the border. Each time you click the mouse a holding point is placed to help maintain the selection. With a clearly defined edge, the Magnetic Lasso can work very well. If the line goes wrong, drag the cursor back over the mistake and press the Backspace. The holding line will be deleted and you can have another go. The accuracy of the tool is adjusted by altering the Feather value in the Tool Options bar. As with most of the selection tools, the Magnetic Lasso takes some practice to perfect. Additionally, using a graphics tablet rather than a mouse will help enormously with the Lasso tools. As with the Marquee tools, selection made with the Lasso tools can be fine-tuned with the Refine Edge dialog (see page 32).

Tip

To improve the Magnetic Lasso's ability to trace the line between the subject and the background, add a temporary Brightness/Contrast adjustment layer and increase the contrast. Once you have completed the selection with the Magnetic Lasso, delete the adjustment layer. The selection will remain in place over the original image layer.

↑↑ The Lasso tool has been used to make a rough selection of the piece of wood. The selection is feathered and brightness increased to bring out detail.

← The contrast between the white wind turbine and the blue sky ensured that the Magnetic Lasso tool was able to identify the subject's edge.

↑ The regular shape of the door is quickly selected using the Polygonal Lasso tool. The color of the door was then adjusted using the Hue/Saturation dialog.

Quick Selection tool

The next two selection tools, the Quick Selection tool and the Magic Wand are found under the Lasso tools in the toolbox. The Quick Selection tool provides an incredibly powerful and intuitive way to make selections, particularly when used in conjunction with the Refine Edge dialog (see

page 32). Introduced in CS3, it works by analyzing the brightness and color of the pixels you initially select, and adds pixels of similar values to make up the selection. The tool is set to automatically add to the selection, and so you can slowly build up the selection using brush strokes. You can

alter the size of the brush in the Tool Options bar. You can also easily paint back over an area to deselect it by holding down the Alt/⌥ key.

1

2

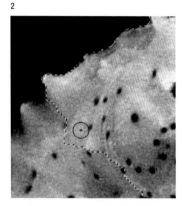

3

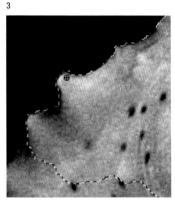

4

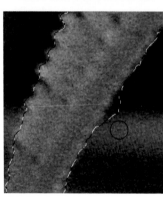

5

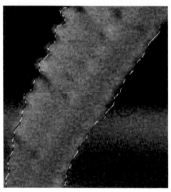

6

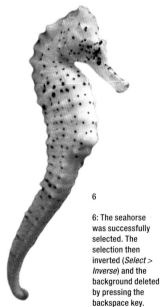

1: Here we're going to use the Quick Selection tool to cut out this irregular-shaped seahorse, which features a variety of colors and tones.

2: Use an appropriate sized brush to start with and paint over the object. Don't go too quickly, as the computer is analyzing the pixels as you paint.

3: For edge details, switch to a smaller brush for a more accurate result.

4 & 5: If the selection goes wrong, simply press the Alt/⌥ key. The "+" symbol turns to a "–" and you can "push" the selection back to the outline.

6: The seahorse was successfully selected. The selection then inverted (*Select > Inverse*) and the background deleted by pressing the backspace key.

Magic Wand

The Magic Wand tool has been around for a while now and under the right circumstances is a very quick and effective way to make a selection. Like the Quick Selection tool, the Magic Wand makes a selection based on brightness and color (which is no doubt why they share the same place in the Toolbox). When you click on a small area of pixels, the Magic Wand selects other pixels with the same (or similar) luminosity values. How close the additionally selected pixels have to be to the initial selection in terms of the luminosity value is determined by the Tolerance setting in the Tool Options bar. The smaller the Tolerance setting, the closer the selected pixels have to be to the "sampled" selection. The Magic Wand really comes into its own when you want to select a large similarly toned area, such as a blue sky or a green car, for example.

As well as adding and subtracting to the selection in the normal way—using the Shift and Alt/⌥ keys—you can also use the Grow, Similar, and Modify commands under the Select menu. Grow adds pixels of similar values, while Similar will select all pixels of similar values, wherever they are in the image.

Under the Modify command, there are additional options: Border, Smooth, Expand, Contract, and Feather. Generally, these work in the same way as the more intuitive Refine Edge dialog (see pages 32–33), but essentially, Expand will increase the selection by the number of pixels you choose, Contract reduces the selection, and Feather softens the edge so you avoid ugly defining lines when making a selection.

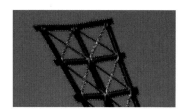

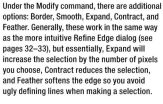

↑ Having made an initial selection of the solid red body of the windmill with the Magic Wand, the smaller blade elements were added by holding down the Shift key. The selection was narrowed (*Select > Modify > Contract*) by 10 pixels, before finally being feathered (*Select > Feather*) by 10 pixels to soften the outline.

↑ In the Magic Wand tool's Options bar you'll find the Tolerance setting. Increasing the Tolerance will make the tool select a wider range of pixel values, resulting in a larger, but less-accurate selection. Reducing the Tolerance will result in a smaller, but more accurate selection.

↑ With the selection made, a cut-out of the windmill was achieved simply by pressing the backspace key.

Refine Edge

Both Photoshop and Photoshop Elements feature the enormously helpful Refine Edge tool. The Refine Edge button becomes available in the Tool Options bar once you've made a selection with any of the Marquee or Lasso tools, the Quick Selection tool, or the Magic Wand. It can also be accessed under the Select menu when an active selection has been made via other selection methods, such as using Color Range (see page 60) or Quick Mask Mode (see page 86). The Refine Edge dialog box is divided into four discrete panels, View Mode, Edge Detection, Adjust Edge, and Output. These are described in more detail below. Together, the various options found in the Refine Edge dialog make it much easier to get an accurate selection.

Refinement brushes

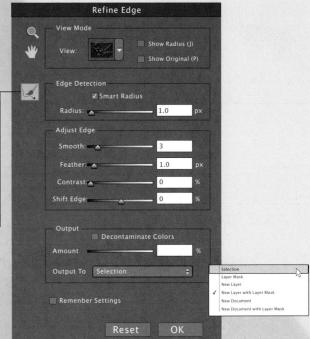

View Mode
The first panel, View Mode, comprises a pull-down menu that offers a number of ways in which you can view your selection. They are pretty self-explanatory, but if you hover over each option with the cursor you'll get a brief description of the option. When checked, the Show Radius option reveals the size of the selection border by temporarily masking out the rest of the selection. The Show Original displays the image without a selection preview.

Edge Detection
Radius: The Radius slider determines the width of the edge selection. Use a narrow radius, such as 1 pixel, for clearly defined, hard-edged objects; use a wider radius for soft-edged objects such as fur or hair. The Smart Radius option analyzes the object and attempts to set the most appropriate Radius.

Refinement brushes: These allow you to increase or decrease the size of the border area depending on whether specific parts of the edge are hard or soft.

Adjust Edge
Smooth: Removes jagged edges from a selection.

Feather: One of the most useful sliders, Feather blurs the selection edge by the number of pixels selected. It's one of the best ways to soften selection edges.

Contrast: This setting sharpens edges and removes fuzzy artifacts between subject and background.

Shift Edge: Physically increases or reduces the size of the selected area. Use this to exclude background pixels from the selection.

Output
The Output panel helps to blend the selection with a new background. The Decontaminate Colors box recolors any stray pixels that are colored differently from those pixels that have been fully selected.

Output To: This pull-down menu provides various ways in which the selection can be saved, such as a selection, a Layer Mask, a new layer, and so on.

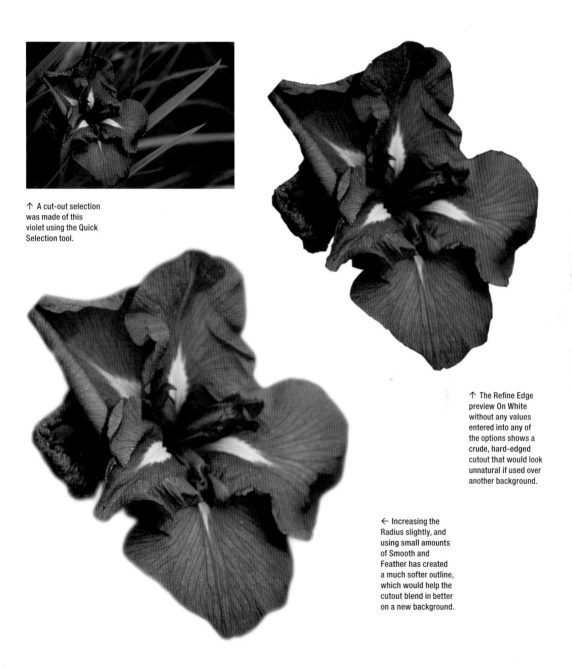

↑ A cut-out selection was made of this violet using the Quick Selection tool.

↑ The Refine Edge preview On White without any values entered into any of the options shows a crude, hard-edged cutout that would look unnatural if used over another background.

← Increasing the Radius slightly, and using small amounts of Smooth and Feather has created a much softer outline, which would help the cutout blend in better on a new background.

Magic Extractor

Under the Image menu in Photoshop Elements you'll find the Magic Extractor tool. This surprisingly effective, semiautomatic extraction tool can remove even quite complex objects from their backgrounds, and is extremely quick and easy to use.

As with all semiautomatic selection tools, some subjects are more successfully isolated than others. Generally, the harder the edge, the cleaner the extraction, but here we're going to use it to extract a dog from its background. Not the easiest selection.

 Foreground brush

 Background brush

 Point Eraser

 Add to Selection

 Remove from Selection

 Smoothing brush

 Zoom tool

Hand tool

To launch Magic Extractor open the image you want to work on and go to Image > Magic Extractor.

The Magic Extractor is a more refined version of the Extract filter that was available in previous versions of Photoshop and Photoshop Elements. It works in a similar way, by analyzing the pixels you select from the object then determining the edge between the object and the background. The major difference between the Magic Extractor and the Extract filter is that the software needs less user input to determine the edge, so making the extraction process much quicker.

1

1: After selecting the Magic Extractor tool, you're presented with a large preview screen that provides you with basic instructions, along with the various tools available to you during the extraction process.

2: Begin by selecting the Foreground brush and roughly draw in the area of the subject you want to extract. Then using the Background brush draw in the area that forms the background.

3: Having marked the foreground and background areas, click the Preview button. Now you can evaluate how well the main subject was extracted from the background. In this case, some of the fine detail in the crown was missed.

4: To tidy up the selection click on the Fill Holes button in the Touch Up panel. This instantly fills in any missing pixels contained within the body of the subject. To add the missing crown details, select the Add to Selection brush and paint in the missing elements. If you go too far you can use the Remove from Selection tool to paint out the background.

5: To soften the edge, Feather the selection. Click Defringe to match the color of any residual background pixels with the foreground pixels. Click OK.

6: After five minutes work with the Magic Extractor, it's possible to obtain an acceptable cutout as seen here.

2

3

4

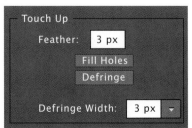

6

5

1

Pen tool

There may be occasions when you need to make a really accurate, clean-edged cutout, particularly if you want to create a photo-montage. To achieve this, the best option is to use the Pen tool and create a Path. Paths in themselves are not selections, but rather outlines. However, you can convert a Path into a selection once you're happy with the outline.

Using the Pen tool takes some practice, particularly with complex shapes. The main feature of Paths are anchor points, which you place every time you click the mouse. If you then click to make the next point, and drag the mouse, two handles will protrude from the anchor point. Moving either one of these handles will cause the line to curve. The idea is to adjust the handles so that the curve accurately follows that of the object you want to cut out. When you've finished creating the outline you can convert the Path into a normal selection.

2

3

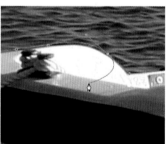

4

5

6

7

8

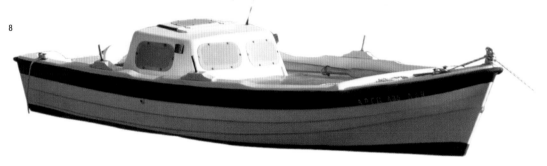

1: In this example, the Pen tool will be used to create a Path around the boat.

2: Zoom right into the image. The first anchor point is placed on part of the outline of the boat. The second point is placed further along the edge. This is a straight line so doesn't require any adjustment, and is simply placed by clicking the mouse. The third point, however, needs to follow the curve of the boat, and so the mouse is dragged pulling the cursor away from the point creating two handles. The bottom handle is dragged until the path neatly follows the curve.

3: Attempting to click on the next point, however, is not possible as the Pen tool automatically continues with the curve.

4: To remedy this, hold down the Alt/⌥ key and click on the previous anchor point. A small "v" shaped symbol will appear next to the Pen tool icon.

5: The next point can now be placed. A straight line will form, but again, dragging the mouse and adjusting the handle will allow you to create another accurate curve.

6: Continue around the boat, clicking the Alt/⌥ key on the previous anchor point whenever you need to create a new line that can be adjusted to follow the outline. You can navigate around the image using the vertical and horizontal sliders at the edge of the screen if necessary. A useful aspect of the Pen tool is that, unlike many of the selection tools, which require you to make the selection at one go, with the Pen tool, you can stop, release the mouse, make a cup of coffee if you like, and return to the path whenever you're ready.

When you get back to the start point, a small "o" will appear next to the anchor point to indicate a completed Path. You can now return to any part of the line that you're not happy with, and using the various tools in the Tool Options bar, add or delete anchor points, reposition them, and so on. Convert the Path by clicking on the "Load path as a selection" icon in the Path's palette. The standard "marching ants" selection will appear.

7: To select the section of water between the boat and the rope, the Polygonal Lasso was used with the Alt/⌥ key held down to deselect that section of the outline selection.

8: You can then use the Refine Edge tool to fine tune the selection.

Raw conversion

All mid-range and enthusiast digital cameras allow you to shoot in what is commonly referred to as the Raw file format. The image file may have a proprietary name, such as NEF for Nikon or CR2 for Canon, but they are still generic Raw files. Shooting Raw has definite advantages.

When you shoot JPEGs, the most common file format, the camera's processor performs a host of operations on the image file, such as increasing color or contrast, sharpening, or even converting the image to black and white, so that it's ready for printing. The camera also compresses the data to a smaller 8-bit file, which although saves space, could result in the loss of potentially important data should you wish to edit the file later in editing software. With Raw files, however, no such processing

occurs. Raw files simply contain the image data as captured by the sensor at the time of shooting. Additionally, being 12- or 14-bit, Raw files contain much more image data than JPEGs, and therefore give you much more data to "play" with when editing. This can be vital if, for example, you want to try to restore blown highlights or reveal detail in dark shadows.

As shooting in Raw has become increasingly popular over time thanks to the improved quality it can bring, more and more photographers are turning to dedicated Raw conversion and workflow software such as Apple's Aperture and Adobe Lightroom as their principal software. But while it's possible to perform an increasing number of editing tasks at a localized level, in terms of "creative image-editing and special

effects" (the principal purpose of this title), you'll still need some form of post-production software. What seems to be emerging for special-effect's work is a workflow in which some of the editing, such as cropping and rotating, setting overall exposure and white balance, and perhaps noise reduction, is undertaken during Raw conversion, while the "creative" side of the editing is completed using post-production software often at pixel level.

Finally, it's worth noting that many "pixel editors," such as Photoshop, Photoshop Elements, and Paint Shop Pro can also process Raw files, although perhaps less efficiently than dedicated Raw conversion software. This means that you don't necessarily have to purchase Raw conversion software to reap the benefits of shooting Raw.

← Adobe's Raw conversion plug-in, known as Adobe Camera Raw (ACR) ships with both Photoshop and Photoshop Elements. If you shoot Raw it's possible to change settings such as White Balance and shooting Profiles from those chosen at the time of shooting, as well as providing adjustments for a whole range of commands, including Exposure, Brightness, Contrast, Saturation, Sharpening, Black-and-White conversion, lens distortion, as well as giving you the chance to do the basics such as remove spots, reduce noise, sharpen, crop and straighten, and apply localized exposure and contrast adjustments. Applying these to the Raw file will not only give the best-quality result once you complete the Raw conversion by opening the file as a JPEG or TIFF in order to print or display the image online, but editing Raw files is a "non-destructive" process. It leaves the Raw data intact, allowing you to return to it later to amend any of the adjustments.

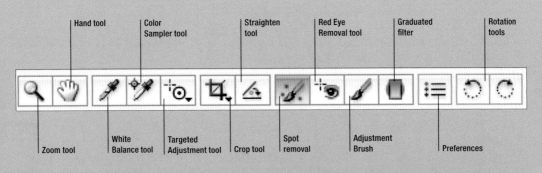

Hand tool

Color
Sampler tool

Straighten
tool

Red Eye
Removal tool

Graduated
filter

Rotation
tools

Zoom tool

White
Balance tool

Targeted
Adjustment tool

Crop tool

Spot
removal

Adjustment
Brush

Preferences

The tools available in Photoshop's ACR plug-in allow you to make a number of corrections and enhancements to Raw files, even at a local level. So although you can't composite images or add special effects using ACR, shooting Raw and optimizing the image in Raw conversion software before exporting to TIFF for further post-production will often yield the best results.

↑ This image has got a number of dust spots due to a dirty sensor. Unfortunately, they are all the more apparent because of the large area of clear blue sky. Selecting the Spot Removal tool in ACR and clicking over the spots makes short work of repairing them. You can leave it up to the software to automatically select a source spot, or alternatively click over the area you want to repair (a red-and-white target circle will appear), and then drag the green-and-white source circle to any area you want to use as a clone. As the process is non-destructive, the spots will still be there on the Raw data, but won't be visible unless you clear the Spot Removal tool.

Adobe Photoshop Lightroom and Apple Aperture are two popular dedicated Raw converters. As well as Raw conversion software, they are also designed to simplify your workflow. During import, images can be given key words, geotagged, updated with personal EXIF data, and placed into named subfolders. Once the images are imported, you can use either software's extensive editing tools to optimize images before printing or saving for the web. Both programs have cataloging software that makes them ideal for photographers who need to process and keep track of large numbers of images.

Thanks to the increasing versatility of such programs, notably with the development of tools such as adjustment brushes that make it possible to amend images at evermore localized levels, an increasing number of photographers are eschewing "pixel editors" such as Photoshop Elements. However, as mentioned earlier, although Raw conversion programs are becoming increasingly versatile, being parametric image editors (that is the amendments you make are recorded as a set of instructions or parameters), they do not edit images in the same way as pixel editors, which alter the actual color and tonal information of every pixel involved in the adjustment. The upside of this is that any editing is nondestructive, so you can always go back to the original image. The downside though for creative editing and special effects is that you can't combine elements of two or more separate images, nor use special effects filters; so for those of you who composite images or utilize special effects plug-ins you'll still need pixel-editing software.

↑ Optimizing Raw files using the numerous editing tools and commands available in Raw workflow software such as Apple's Aperture will ensure that you have the best possible image quality before proceeding with any additional post-production.

↑ Lightroom's toolset is comparable to that of Aperture. The biggest advance in more recent versions of both programs is the evolution of their respective Adjustment brushes. These allow you to select specific areas of an image, and then make localized adjustments to settings such as exposure, brightness, contrast, saturation, and sharpness. The tools are surprisingly versatile and offer a great deal of control over the image.

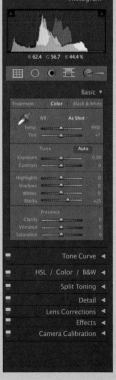

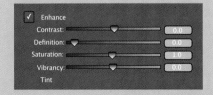

2

Image Enhancement

Image resolution versus image size

300ppi

← It's an image's resolution (measured in pixels per inch, or ppi) that determines how it will appear when printed. At 300ppi the image appears as a continuous tone photograph, reduce the resolution to 30ppi, however, and immediately the image appears blocky, or pixelated.

30ppi

A fair amount of confusion often emerges when the discussion turns to image size and resolution. It's important to know the terminology and to understand the constraints imposed on you when resizing an image if you want to ensure a good result.

All digital photographs are made up of a specific number of pixels—the number being determined by the number of photosites or receptors on the camera's sensor. For example, an 18-megapixel camera will be able to record images with a maximum pixel count of 18 million (give or take a few). These may, for the sake of convenience, be distributed as 5,000 pixels along the bottom and 3,600 up the side—

$5,000 \times 3,600 = 18,000,000$. So far, so good. The confusion, however, usually arises when you want to know how large prints can be from an image file with these pixel dimensions. This is where resolution comes in. Resolution is measured in pixels per inch (ppi), and setting an image's resolution will determine the size the individual pixels are viewed at. The industry standard resolution for printed photographs is 300ppi. With 300 pixels crammed into 1 inch it's impossible to make out the individual pixels, thus making photographs appear smooth and continuous in tone. An image, therefore, with pixel dimensions of 5000×3600 set at a resolution of 300ppi would make

a print with dimensions of 16.6×12 inches. However, 300ppi is an industry standard, and for home printing you may find, after running a couple of tests, that with your printer you can't tell the difference between photographs printed at 300ppi or 200ppi. In which case the physical size of our example image, printed at 200ppi, could increase to 20×15 inches, or perhaps more significantly you could make a closer crop without degrading the print.

As far as publishing images to be viewed on screen is concerned, you only need to set a much lower resolution of around 72–96 ppi for the images to appear continuous as tone.

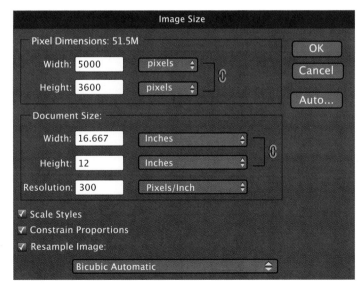

← Photoshop's Image Size dialog box (*Image > Image Size*) provides information about the image's physical dimensions (here 5000 × 3600 pixels), its file size (51.5 Mb), the existing resolution (300ppi) and the physical size of the image when printed at that resolution (16.6 × 12 inches).

The pull-down menus allow you to change the units the measurements are given in. For example, if you're more comfortable thinking of the document size in centimeters rather than inches, you can select "cm" from the pull-down menu.

Resizing an image

With many digital cameras now boasting sensors with 18 or more megapixels, the issue of resizing images upward is less significant than it used to be in the early days of digital photography, when the pixel count for many cameras used to be 3 megapixels. In those early days, to get an A4 print it was necessary to rescale an image using a process known as interpolation. Today, however, A4-sized prints are achievable from most cameras without recourse to interpolation.

However, the question of upscaling does still arise from time to time—as does the issue of downsizing for the web.

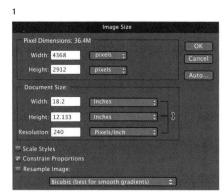

1

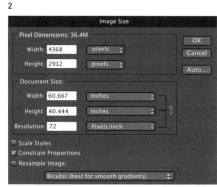

2

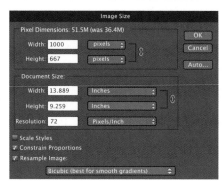

3   4

1: To begin resizing an image for the web, go to *Image > Image Size*. This image was taken with a 12-megapixel camera, which has produced an image with dimensions 4368 x

2912 pixels with a size of 36.4Mb—far too big to upload to the internet.

2: Let's see what happens if we change the resolution to the web-friendly 72ppi.

Because of the relationship between resolution and print size, all we have managed to achieve is to increase the document size in terms of inches (but note that neither the

pixel dimensions nor the resolution nor the file size have changed).

3: So just by changing the resolution we don't affect the image data at all. To reduce the amount of data

and therefore the file size, we need to check the Resample Image box. Now reducing the resolution brings a massive reduction in both the image and file size. However,

1310 pixels is still too large, as is 3.28Mb.

4: With the Resample Image box still checked, let's reduce the pixel width to 1000. This will fit neatly on most

5

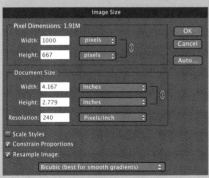

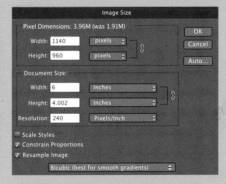

6

monitors. We're getting close to a workable size now.

5: To complete the resizing, go to *File > Save for Web & Devices*. Here you can fine tune the

resizing using the various quality settings in the top right-hand part of the screen. With the settings shown here we've reduced our image to an acceptable 68.9K,

and the preview of the image shows acceptable image quality. The Progressive box enables a quick preview of the image to display before gradually

becoming sharper as the image redraws.

6: To upscale an image, again you need to check the Resample Image box. Choose Bicubic Smoother in the

bottom pull-down menu. If you know what dimensions you want to achieve simply enter these into the relevant document size box. Here we've increased this image to 6

inches wide. Note the increased file size. Upsizing (or interpolating) should be avoided if at all possible as the image quality of the finished result is difficult to control.

Cropping

Very few of us, when shooting conventional 35mm film—particularly color—had access to the photographic equipment needed for cropping images (at least assuming we wanted to enlarge the cropped area to the original size). We had to frame our photos with great care or live with the consequences. If we captured the image with a large expanse of uninteresting foreground, or an unsightly sign in the background, there was nothing to be done, other than go to an expensive professional photo lab and pay for a cropped print.

Of course we should still aim to frame accurately and effectively in-camera today, but cropping is now a standard editing task in the digital environment. All editing programs have crop tools, though some are more sophisticated than others.

It's also important to think of cropping as a creative process and not simply one that conveniently gets rid of unwanted elements of a scene. Certain formats, such as the square, work better with certain types of images and can really show an image off to its best advantage.

↑ To make a straight-forward crop, select the Crop tool from the Toolbox. Assess the image you're going to crop and think about the shape you want the final image to be. Here a square or even portrait crop would have worked successfully, but for the purposes of the layout in which the image appeared, it had to remain a landscape picture. Click at the point where you want the crop to start and drag over the image area with the crop tool. The standard marching ants selection line will appear. If you're happy with the crop, click the Commit transform button (a tick symbol in the Tool Options bar in the case of Photoshop and Photoshop Elements) or press the Return key. The finished image has much of the unwanted background removed.

← You can alter the shape of the crop before committing to it. Once you've released the Crop tool and made the initial crop, a bounding box with eight handles will appear. You can click and drag the handles to alter the shape of the crop to any format you want. Here, a portrait format was chosen.

← This image has plenty of character, but may be more powerful as a squared-up portrait. Select the Crop tool in the Toolbox, and in the Tool Options bar select Size and Resolution in the drop-down menu.

Now you can directly dial in dimensions and resolution in the dialog box. We want a square shot for print, in which case dimensions have been set to 10 × 10in and the resolution to 300ppi.

← With specific dimensions used in the Tool Options bar, now when you drag the Crop tool, the crop will automatically conform to the input dimensions, in this case a square. You can select as much or as little of the image—if necessary Photoshop will interpolate the crop to obtain the 300ppi resolution, although the more the software has to interpolate the poorer the image quality. It's also possible to move the crop by clicking the cursor within the bounding box and moving the crop over another area of the image.

Cropping

Rotating

A common mistake we all make from time to time is not paying enough attention to any horizontal lines that appear in the shot—the most common being the horizon—which when we come to view them later on-screen are not straight. Many digital cameras have optional grids that can be turned on in the viewfinder to help us keep horizontals straight, but every so often we're bound to come across an image that needs to be rotated. Fortunately it's a quick and easy editing task. Here's just one way (there are a number) of rotating an image to ensure horizontals are straight.

1

2

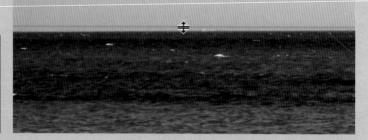

Tip

If you change your mind before confirming either a crop or a rotation, you can either press the Cancel button, which is next to the confirm button on the Tool Options bar or simply press the Esc key.

1: A quick glance of this shot of a kitesurfer, and the horizon appears pretty much straight. However, with any image that has such a clearly defined horizon, it's always a good idea to be certain before progressing too far with further editing.

2: With the Move tool selected, it's possible to click on the top ruler (go to *View > Show Rulers* if you can't see it) and drag a horizontal line down to align with the horizon in the image. Here we can see that the ocean line is slightly higher on the right side.

3

4

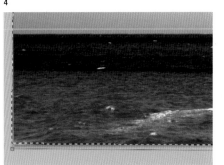

3: To rotate the image, go to *Select > All* (Ctrl/⌘ + A). The marching ants will appear around the edges of the image. Next go to *Edit > Transform > Rotate* (Ctrl/⌘ + T). Move the cursor outside the image area and place it close to one of the corners. The rotation cursor will appear. Move the cursor up or down (in this case down) to align the horizon with the horizontal rule.

4: When you're sure the image is straight, release the mouse. However, before committing to the adjustment, use the handles of the bounding box to pull the image out to cover the white canvas that will have appeared when it was rotated. Be sure you don't visibly distort the image if you have to cover large areas of white. To remove the horizontal rule, choose the Move tool, click on the line, and move it up to the top of the frame.

5

5: Once you've covered any white background canvas areas, press the Return key, or click the Commit Transform (green checkmark) icon.

Fixing converging verticals

Photographing a tall building from ground level usually involves pointing the camera upward in order to fit as much of the building as possible in the frame. However, when you come to view the picture later, you'll notice that the top of the building is narrower than the bottom. This is due to converging verticals. It's the same effect as looking along a straight road and seeing it narrow to a single point in the distance, only with verticals you're looking up rather than along. Traditionally, photographers used tilt-shift lenses to counter this, but these are very costly. It's much less expensive to use editing software.

1

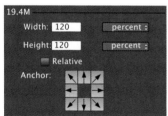

2

1: To get as much as possible of this view of Budapest reflected in the Ritz hotel, the camera had to be pointed upward, resulting in the common problem of converging verticals, made all the more obvious due to the uniform structure of the modern hotel building.

2: To fix the problem, the first thing to do is to increase the background canvas so you have additional space to work in. Go to *Image > Canvas Size*, select "percent" from the pull-down value menu and increase the width and height by 120 percent. Next, using the Rectangular Marquee tool draw a selection around the visible image.

3

4

5

3: To help you align the verticals, go to *View > Show > Grid*. Now let's turn to the verticals. Selecting *Edit > Transform > Perspective* will place points around the selection. Dragging either of the top points sideways will result in the opposite side extending by the same amount. Keep dragging until the verticals align with the grid. Click the Commit transform button in the Tool Options bar, but don't deselect the selection.

4: Next go to *Edit > Transform > Distort* and drag the middle boundary point up slightly. This adds the small amount of height that the image lost when you corrected the verticals. Be sure not to over stretch the image. Look for any elements in the picture, such as circles or people, that will help you to judge you have the correct vertical proportions.

5: When you're happy with the correction, press the Return key. Now all that remains is to select the Crop tool and square the image. You will lose a certain amount of the image when you crop, but this is unavoidable.

Fixing lens distortion

Modern lenses are designed and manufactured to exacting standards, and most will produce very good to excellent image quality, depending on their cost. However, the increasing popularity of zoom lenses, particularly super zooms, which optically provide many more challenges for lens manufacturers than prime or fixed focal length lenses, means that we are still often confronted with two common lens distortion issues—pin-cushion and barrel. Pin-cushion distortion tends to occur at the telephoto end of a zoom lens and results in a pinched look to an image. The effect is usually most obvious in images that have strong vertical lines—the lines appear to curve inward toward the center. Barrel distortion is the opposite, and is usually associated with zoom lenses used at wide-angle settings. Again, the distortion is most apparent in images with vertical lines, which bulge outward toward the edges. Fortunately, with Photoshop's Lens Correction filter both issues are easily solved.

1

1: This photograph was taken with a 70–200mm zoom lens, set at its longest focal length, and the image then cropped. Although the brick walls either side of the doorway are fairly old and not particularly straight, there is distinct pin-cushion distortion, most noticeable on the left side of the photograph.

2: To access Photoshop's Lens Correction filter go to *Filter > Lens Correction...*

The image will appear in a large preview window. To the right of the window are the various commands available to the Lens Correction tool. To help with any alignment issues, ensure that the grid is turned on by clicking the Show Grid button at the bottom of the screen.

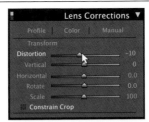

← Lightroom also has a database of lens profiles that will automatically correct lens issues if selected. But, again, if a lens isn't listed there are a number of manual adjustments that you can make to address problems such as distortion and converging verticals (see page 52–53).

2

Photoshop holds the profiles of a number of popular lenses. If your lens is listed, try the Auto Correction feature to fix distortion, chromatic aberration, and vignetting. If your lens isn't listed click Custom. To fix distorion use the Remove Distortion slider. Moving the slider to the right (toward the pin-cushion icon) introduces pin-cushion distortion to the image, negating any barrel effect. In the example here, however, we're going to move the slider toward the barrel icon to remove the pin-cushioning. As you move the slider, compare any vertical lines in the image with those of the grid. Keep moving the slider until the verticals are as straight as possible.

3: Usually the distortion only requires a relatively small correction value. Here, the uneven wall on the left made it difficult to judge when the distortion had been corrected, but the wall on the right and the bars in front of the door now look sufficiently straight.

3

Correcting chromatic aberration

Another issue that can be addressed with the Lens Correction filter is chromatic aberration. Chromatic aberration occurs when the lens is unable to focus light of different wavelengths—in other words colors—on the same focal plane. The result is areas of discoloration. These are most noticeable around high-contrasting edges (hence the phenomenon is also known as "color fringing"), and is more likely to occur at the edges of wide-angle shots. Chromatic aberration can occur with even the most expensive lenses under certain circumstances, but is more likely and more apparent with cheaper glass.

Chromatic aberration is a lens distortion issue that can be addressed in Lightroom using the Raw file. As any corrections you make using Lightroom are non-destructive, it makes sense to correct the issue at this stage before opening the file as a TIFF or JPEG. That way you'll be making the best use of Raw's extra data.

← Photographed with a compact camera, and with the lens set at EFL 34mm, the chromatic aberration in this shot is not too apparent. However, on closer inspection it's possible to detect some color fringing on the edges of the branches, particularly those set against the blue background of the sky, as shown by the inset picture.

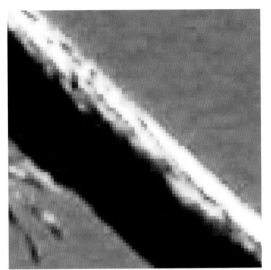

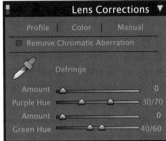

← Again we're going to turn to the Lens Correction filter to get rid of the ugly color fringing. It's worth experimenting with all the sliders to see what impact they have on the image. In this example, adjustments to the Red/Cyan and Blue/Yellow Fringes sliders improved the shot.

Lightroom features an automatic chromatic aberration control, but if that doesn't fix the problem there are a number of powerful manual options.

← At this size the final image doesn't look too different from the uncorrected version. However, with a larger print the chromatic aberration may well have been visible and spoilt the image.

Color adjustments

There could be any number of reasons why you may feel it necessary to adjust the colors in an image. It might be that you simply want to boost the overall color of an image for a more saturated look;

alternatively you may want to single out one particular color to increase or decrease saturation without affecting the rest of the colors in the image. Whatever color adjustment you want

to make, you'll get the best results using the Hue/Saturation command. This is a powerful tool that lets you make color changes quickly and easily.

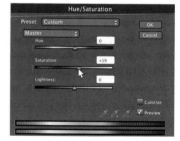

← When you choose your camera's user settings, it's advisable to set the color saturation control to a minimum, unless you're intending to print directly from the camera. Although this will usually result in images that lack color right out of the camera, it does mean that you can color correct the image in a much more controlled manner using image-editing software, rather than relying on your camera's processor to get it right for you.

Once the camera has embedded the color settings, it's often difficult to change them should you want to—especially if you're shooting JPEGs—without degrading the image. Here a Hue/Saturation command was used and the Saturation slider moved to the right to boost the overall color. A fairly strong setting was used to make the most of the warm reds of the sunset.

1

2

1: This photograph of fishing boats has attractive, nicely saturated colors, but the yellow nets in the foreground are not as vivid as they seemed at the time of shooting.

2: If we increase the overall saturation of the image so that the nets are brighter, the result is distinctly oversaturated colors across the board. Not the result we want.

3

Hue/Saturation

Preset:	Custom		OK
Yellows			Cancel
Hue:		0	
Saturation:		+34	
Lightness:		0	

□ Colorize
☑ Preview

15°/45°   75°\105°

3: One of the benefits of the Hue/Saturation command is that you can select specific colors to enhance using the pull-down menu. By selecting "Yellows" we can increase the saturation of the yellow hues in the image without oversaturating the rest of the image.

4

HSL / Color / B&W ▼

Red
Hue — 0
Saturation — 0
Luminance — 0

Orange
Hue — 0
Saturation — 0
Luminance — 0

Yellow
Hue — 0
Saturation — 0
Luminance — 0

Green
Hue — 0
Saturation — 0
Luminance — 0

Aqua
Hue — 0
Saturation — 0
Luminance — 0

4: If you're working with Raw files, Lightroom offers a powerful color control panel that features three sliders—Hue, Saturation, and Luminence—for each of the key eight colors—Red, Orange, Yellow, Green, Aqua, Blue, Purple, and Magenta. The sliders let you target specific color adjustments with accuracy.

Fine-tuning color

Although the Hue/Saturation dialog is a powerful and relatively versatile tool, when it comes to making really specific color corrections it's necessary to use the command in combination with other tools. In this example, we need to select and correct a very specific color without affecting any of the other colors in the photograph. This is a good example of a very localized correction that simply would not be possible to accomplish using a Raw conversion program.

← This striking image of a humming-bird hawkmoth in flight has captured the insect well. However, the Valerian on which it is feeding appears too red (perhaps reflected light from a red colored wall). The Hue/Saturation command on its own will not be able to isolate the color of the plant as it is a mixture of a number of subtle hues.

↓ Instead, we select the Eyedropper tool from the Toolbox and click on a particularly red part of the plant. Having sampled the color, we'll next go to Select > Color Range. This brings up the Color Range dialog box. This shows all the elements of the picture that share the sampled color in white. Moving the Fuzziness slider to the right will widen the selection. Here we've set the slider so that most of the plant has been selected.

← Having set the Fuzziness slider, clicking OK will make the selection, outlined by the familiar marching ants.

↑ Now that we've isolated the offending color, we can use the Hue/Saturation command to change the color of the selected area. Hiding the marching ants selection by pressing Ctrl/⌘ + H provides us with a clear view of the plant as we're making the adjustment.

← Experimenting with various Hue settings, and reducing the saturation a little, provides us with a much more accurate color— important to keep the botanists happy!

Using the Color Range command is an excellent way of selecting an area of an image for corrections other than just color.

Dodging & burning

Dodging and burning are old darkroom terms and involve making specific areas of an image either lighter (dodging) or darker (burning). In the days of black-and-white printing, the dodging and burning process was considered a fundamental creative process in order to arrive at the final printed result.

Conventionally, dodging was carried out by masking certain areas of the print so they would receive less light as the photo was being exposed, thereby making them lighter.

Other areas that received additional light during exposure became darker

when the print was developed—and these areas were said to be "burned" or "burned in."

Using the digital Dodge and Burn tools has the same effect, but they are much easier to control, and you can always go back a step if you don't like the result.

← This photograph of ferns was shot in dappled sunlight, with light scattered by the canopy of the tree's leaves. The fern shows up quite brightly against the relatively dark bark of the tree behind, but we can use the Dodge and Burn tools to emphasize the effect.

↓ With the Burn tool selected, a fairly strong exposure was set in the Tool Options bar, and the Range kept to the default Midtones. Next, with an appropriately sized brush, the Burn tool was painted over the trunk of the tree to darken it.

   Range: Midtones ⇕ Exposure: 27% ▼   ✓ Protect Tones

↓ Once all the areas that needed darkening were burned in, the Burn tool was replaced by the Dodge tool. Similar values were set in the Tool Options bar, and another brush size selected, which covered just the ferns.

→ It's better to Dodge and Burn gradually, making several passes over the relevant areas. That way you remain in control of the adjustment. The finished result picks out the fern, making it stand out against the backdrop.

Tip

You'll find you'll get much better results using the Dodge and Burn tools with images in 16-bit mode. So don't convert any images you've opened as Raw files into JPEGs (or reduce them to 8-bit) if you're intending to use these tools.

Alternatively use the Adjustment brush in Lightroom or Aperture and adjust the exposure to lighten or darken selected parts of the image.

Noise in a digital image is caused by interference within the camera's sensor. When the sensor is used at low sensitivity settings, such as ISO 100 or 200, noise is rarely noticeable. And with some digital SLRs, even high ISO settings of 1600+ will result in little appreciable noise. However, with compact cameras, because sensors are smaller and therefore more prone to interference, high ISO settings, often used in low light to obtain a faster shutter speed, will produce images with poor noise artifacts. These manifest themselves as discolored, grain-like blotches, which are usually most noticeable in shadow regions. In really bad examples, noise can ruin a photograph altogether. In such extreme circumstances little can be done to retrieve the image, but in less extreme cases, most image-editing applications will have a filter that can at least improve the situation a little.

← Taken in very poor lighting with a high ISO setting, this detail of a shot of Prague's rooftops shows just how much noise there is present in the image.

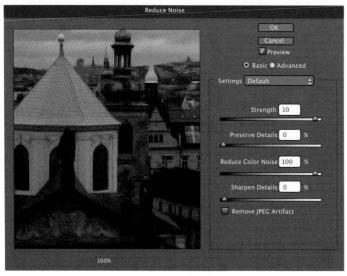

← Going to *Filter > Noise > Reduce Noise* brings up the Reduce Noise dialog box. Experimenting with the Default settings will give you a good idea as to how the filter works. Here, setting the Strength and Reduce Color Noise to maximum does a good job of getting rid of all the noise, but the image has lost too much detail and looks plastic.

← You have to experiment with the various settings to find a compromise between noise and acceptable loss of detail. Here, reducing Strength and Color Noise, and introducing some Preserve and Sharper Details has given us the optimal result.

Noise Reduction

Luminance	0
Detail	50
Contrast	0
Color	25
Detail	50

↑ If you shoot Raw you have the option of using ACR or a Raw conversion program to reduce noise. Software developers have been working hard to improve the automatic demosaicing processing of Raw editors, and the results can be extremely good. Lightroom's Noise Reduction pane allows you to target Luminance and Color noise separately. Luminance noise creates the grayscale speckled effect often seen in noisy images, while Color or "chroma" noise causes the ugly discoloration. Increasing both settings will result in a less noisy, but more plasticky looking image, which can be offset by the Detail sliders.

Sharpening

There are many reasons why an image may not be as sharp as you'd like. In some cases it could simply be that lack of sharpness is due to a small focusing error at the time the photo was taken, resulting in an image that is slightly soft. Alternatively, the lens used may not have been able to resolve all the detail in the scene as accurately as you'd have liked. In other cases, it may be that you shoot Raw with no in-camera sharpening to counteract the softening effect of the camera's antialiasing filter and demosaicing process.

Sharpening should take place at two or three stages along the imaging workflow. The first stage is often referred to as "presharpening" or capture sharpening. This can take place automatically when the camera converts the image to a JPEG and applies its own sharpening algorithms. Alternatively, it can be applied manually during Raw conversion. The purpose of presharpening is to sharpen an image rendered soft by the filter and demosaicing process mentioned earlier. The second stage is "creative sharpening," at which point you might decide to sharpen specific areas of an image, while leaving others soft, such as the eyes in a portrait. The final stage is "output sharpening." This occurs at the end of the editing process, and is intended to show the image with optimum sharpness depending on final usage—such as print or web.

1: Whenever you open an image in your image software, it's impossible to tell whether or not it's really sharp until you zoom into it and view it 100% or at Actual Pixels. On initial viewing this image looks pretty sharp.

2: Going to *View > Actual Pixels*, however, reveals that this is in fact quite a soft image. We can probably tease out quite a lot more detail with appropriately applied tools.

3

Sharpening		
Amount		6
Radius		1.0
Detail		16
Masking		79

Detail		
Sharpening		
Amount		25
Radius		1.0
Detail		25
Masking		0

4

3: Recent versions of ACR and Lightroom have improved sharpening features, found under the Detail tab. The Amount slider controls the strength of the sharpening effect. The Radius slider determines how many pixels around the edge are affected. The higher the Radius number the more pixels are affected, and the greater the sharpening. However, it's the Radius slider that is primarily responsible for the ugly halo effect you sometimes see with oversharpened images, so start with a low value. The Detail slider increases the contrast between affected pixels. It works well in areas with detail, but introduce too much and areas of flat color will degrade. This can be remedied by increasing the Masking setting. Masking localizes the other sharpening values by applying them only to the edges. A zero value applies no mask, meaning the entire image is affected; increasing the Masking reduces the number of pixels affected. A value of 100 means sharpening is only being applied to the most contrasting edges.

4: Using the values shown above, much more apparent detail in these flying cows is created than before.

High Pass sharpening

High Pass sharpening combines a background layer with a duplicate layer on which Photoshop's High Pass filter has been applied—hence the name of this particular sharpening technique.

It's an extremely powerful technique, producing a strong sharpening effect, and for this reason it is often used when a photograph needs to be sharpened for output to a printer. One of the

benefits of High Pass sharpening when compared with many other sharpening techniques, such as using the Unsharp Mask, is that it doesn't sharpen artifacts such as noise.

↑ This shot of the famous French landmark, Le Mont St. Michel, is quite soft, as shown by the inset. We could use the Unsharp Mask filter to sharpen the image, but with a lot of plain sky in the image, this might introduce artifacts to the photograph.

→ To begin the High Pass sharpening routine, duplicate the background layer (*Layer > Duplicate Layer*), and call it High Pass.

↓ With the High Pass layer selected go to *Filter > Other > High Pass*. In the High Pass dialog box, set a Radius of 10 pixels.

↓ Return to the Layers palette, and select Hard Light from the Blending Mode pull-down menu. Ensuring that you're viewing the image at 100%, fine tune the sharpening effect by clicking on the Opacity slider and reducing it until you're happy with the result.

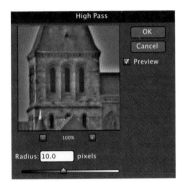

↓ The final version has been sharpened quite considerably, without introducing any sharpening artifacts into the sky.

The Smart Sharpen filter was introduced with Photoshop CS2, and subsequently in Photoshop Elements as Adjust Sharpness. It replaces Photoshop's popular Unsharp Mask filter as the main sharpening tool of choice as it is able to apply different sharpening effects depending on the root cause of the photograph's focus problem.

Generally there are three reasons why an image may not be in focus. The first two occur when the photograph is taken—either inaccurate focus or camera shake. The third is digital blurring, such as softening applied to an image by the camera processor or Raw processor as part of the demosaicing process (the conversion from the patterned color information that the sensor records to the full color image seen on the display). The Smart Sharpen filter is able to deal with these individually, unlike the Unsharp Mask filter, which applied a Gaussian Blur mask to an entire image. The latter occasionally can create more problems than it solves.

↑↑ The lettering on the signs of this soap stall in a French market reveal the lack of focus in this image. Going to *Filter > Sharpen > Smart Sharpen* brings up the Smart Sharpen dialog. In this particular example, we need to get rid of lens blur and so Lens Blur was selected from the Remove pull-down menu.

↑ Applying quite a high Radius amount, when compared with the Radius values we usually select with the Unsharp Mask Filter has sharpened the lettering (and the rest of the image), but has not introduced any ugly sharpening artifacts.

↑ Using a relatively slow shutter speed to take this shot of a French market has resulted in motion blur. We can remove the worst effects of the blur by selecting Motion Blur in the Remove pull-down menu. You'll need to experiment with the Angle setting to find the value that best removes the blur.

→ The Gaussian Blur option in the Remove pull-down menu works in the same way as the traditional Unsharp Mask filter. It's designed to sharpen images that appear slightly soft when viewed straight out of the camera, even though they are in focus.

3

Image Retouching

If you use a digital SLR and frequently change lenses, sooner or later you're bound to discover dust on your camera's sensor. Dust spots are most apparent in areas of uniform color, such as a clear blue sky, and when you use a narrow aperture setting, such as $f/22$ or $f/32$. The dust manifests itself as dark spots on the image. Fortunately, most image-editing software can make short work of removing dust spots, and of course you can apply the same tools to removing freckles and moles.

← ← Choose the Spot Healing Brush tool from the Toolbox. In the Tool Options bar, make sure the selected brush is set to 100% Hardness; this ensures the correction is kept to the localized area around the dust spot. Zoom into the area with the dust spot, and adjust the diameter of the brush using the "[" and "]" keys until it closely encircles the spot.

← Simply click the mouse and the spot disappears.

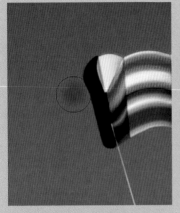

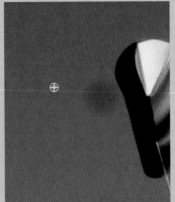

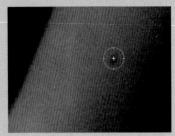

Spot Edit: Clone | Heal

Size   ————————●——— 76
Radius —————————————▲ 100

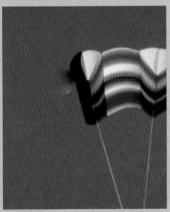

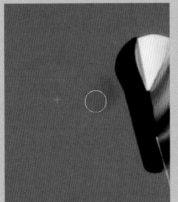

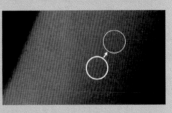

↑↑ The Spot Healing Brush tool works by sampling pixels nearby. Problems arise therefore, if the spot is located near to an object that does not match the background.

↑ Attempting to use the Spot Healing Brush tool on the spot next to the kite has resulted in an inappropriate sample. The spot has been replaced by pixels sampled from the kite and not the sky.

↑↑ In such situations you need to turn to the Clone Stamp tool. Place the cursor on an appropriate area of sky. Press the Alt/⌥ key (the cursor will change into a cross within a circle) and click the mouse to sample the area. Using a harder brush allows you to get closer to the edge of the kite.

↑ Move the cursor over the spot and begin to paint over it with the sampled pixels. For the best results it's good practice to change the sample area periodically, particularly if there is some texture present in the image.

↑ Lightroom's Spot Removal tool is quick and intuitive. Simply place the tool over the spot (here a small skin mole) and click. Lightroom automatically samples a nearby area of skin and replaces the target area. You can

manually move the source area (click H to reveal). The Heal setting blends the target area with surrounding pixels. Use the Clone setting to replace the target area with precisely the pixels from the source areas.

Bright light reflecting off any shiny surface can cause what are commonly referred to as hotspots. Hotspots are usually seen on skin in a studio situation, where the bright, intense lights reflect off even only very slightly greasy skin—this is why make-up artists always carry around large pots of powder to puff onto people's faces. However, hotspots can also occur outside studio situations, particularly under shade in sunny conditions, when the odd beam of sunshine can cause a light patch of skin to overexpose.

← This portrait has some nice features. The gaze is direct, the expression inscrutable, and there is some good bokeh in the background. However, the cheek facing the sun is overexposed, and spoils the shot.

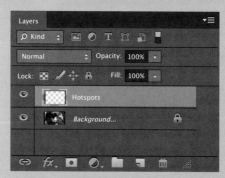

← Go to *Layer > New > Layer...* (Shift + Ctrl/⌘ + N) to create a new blank layer. Call it "Hotspots."

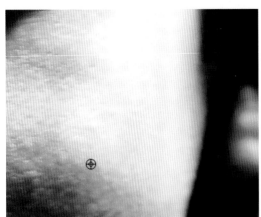

↑ Select the Clone tool from the Toolbox and in the Tool Options bar set Mode to Darken and reduce the Opacity. This will ensure that any adjustments will only affect the pixels that are lighter than the surrounding area. Also make sure that the Sample pull-down menu is set to All Layers.

← Select a source point by holding down the Alt/⌥ key and clicking on the piece of skin nearest to the hotspot that shares the same tone. Sample the skin and gradually cover the hotspot. Remember to work slowly, and use the visibility eye in the new layer to check your corrections—it's very easy to go too far and make the skin look unnatural. Try to blur the new layer slightly to soften the effect.

↓ The patched skin drastically improves the photo. Go to *Layer > Flatten Image* before outputting.

Dust spots and minor skin blemishes are one thing, but supposing you wanted to remove a much larger and more complicated object? The secret is to combine a number of the cloning tools you have at your disposal, and make use of the keyboard buttons "[" and "]" as well as the Tool Options bar so the tools you do employ are working at their best.

1: This fun festival shot has a captivating main subject in an interesting pose, but the stilt coming out from under his cloak draws attention.

Removing it would transform a regular carnival shot into a surreal snapshot, defying the laws of gravity.

1

2

3

4

5

6

6: The finished image attracts attention and invites further study—which makes it all the more important to be fastidious in your cloning of the area underneath the cloak.

2: To start the transformation, make a selection—using any of the methods discussed previously with which you feel comfortable—of just the stilt at the bottom right of the image. Try to be precise, but it doesn't have to be perfect—yet.

3: To fill in the selected area, begin by using an excellent and advanced (but easy-to-use) feature, found in Photoshop CS5 onward called Content-Aware Fill. Go to Edit > Fill and select Content-Aware in the Contents Use pull-down menu. Photoshop will replace the object with areas of pixels that match the background. The success of the tool varies depending on the image and the object, but it saves a lot of time by doing an approximate job first, which can then be touched up the old-fashioned way.

4: Switch to the Clone tool, and carefully sample random areas of the gravel to fill in the distorted areas filled in by the Content Aware algorithm. Randomizing the selected areas avoids any obvious repeated patterns, and particularly works on large even-toned areas such as the street—but be sure to take into account the different shade between the shaded and sunlit patches.

5: To complete the effect, you can also just barely separate the left side of the cloak from the ground, by cloning in a thin line of brighter street, sampled from the sunlit areas. Switching the brush to Lighten helps define your area and avoid cloning over areas you've already touched up. Starting with a definitive line and gradually expanding it is a good working method.

Softening skin

The retouching and cloning tools can be put to good use in portrait photography in a variety of ways. We've seen how skin blemishes such as freckles, moles, and spots can be quickly eradicated with the Spot Removal tool, here we're going to use some other tools and methods to soften a subject's skin without losing sharpness and definition in the essential element of a portrait—the eyes.

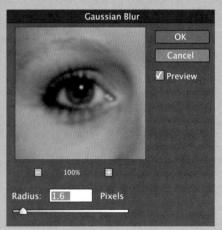

↑ Very little make-up has been used for this softly lit portrait. The result is a very pleasing, natural-looking shot, but the pores and some very minor blemishes are apparent on the model's skin.

↑ Open the Gaussian Blur filter (*Filter > Blur > Gaussian Blur*) and increase the Radius until the skin appears softer and smoother. Here only a small radius was needed. If you wanted to cover over more significant blemishes—such as acne or patches of very dry skin—increase the radius.

←← Next, open the History palette (*Window > History*) and select the Open history state.

← With the Open history state selected, click in the empty box in the Gaussian Blur history state to add a History Brush.

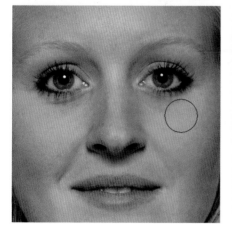

↑↑ Select the History Brush tool from the Toolbar, and in the Tool Options bar, be sure that the Mode is set to Lighten. Painting will then only affect pixels darker than the Gaussian Blur state.

↑ With an appropriately sized History Brush begin to paint over the model's face. You will see the skin soften as you paint.

→ The finished result shows a softer complexion, but without the loss of detail in the eyes or hair.

Enhancing teeth & eyes

With the eyes being the most significant feature in a portrait, you want them to really stand out. One of the simplest ways to do this is to whiten them. And if you're whitening the eyes, it makes sense to whiten the teeth at the same time. Finally, there's also a very quick way to add a little extra sparkle to the eyes. As always with portrait enhancement, the key is not to go too far.

1: With such a direct gaze and the teeth visible in this portrait, it's only a matter of moments to brighten the image by whitening the eyes and teeth a little. Begin by duplicating the Background layer (*Layer > Duplicate Layer*, or press Ctrl/⌘ + J). Call the new layer "Eyes."

2: Choose the Dodge tool from the Toolbox, and in the Tool Options bar set Exposure to around 20% and the Range to Midtones.

3: Zoom right into the first eye, choose a small, fairly hard brush, and paint over the white of the eye. Repeat the exercise on the other eye.

4: When you've completed the eyes, turn your attention to the teeth. Don't worry about whitening everything too much at this stage.

1

2

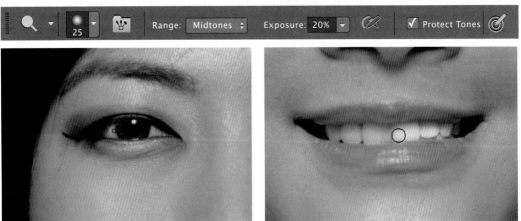

3

4

5

6

5: When you've whitened the eyes and teeth, zoom out to assess the portrait. Here it's clear the whitening is overdone and looks very unnatural.

6: Go to the Layers palette and select the Eyes layer. Drag the Opacity slider to the left until the eyes and teeth look brighter, but natural.

7: With the teeth and eyes whitened it's time to add a little more sparkle to the eyes.

Burn (Darken)
Dodge (Lighten)
Iris Enhance
Soften Skin
Teeth Whitening

If you're working in Raw, Lightroom has a dedicated Teeth Whitening setting associated with the Adjustment brush. Other portrait retouching options include Soften Skin and Iris Enhance.

7

Enhancing teeth & eyes

8

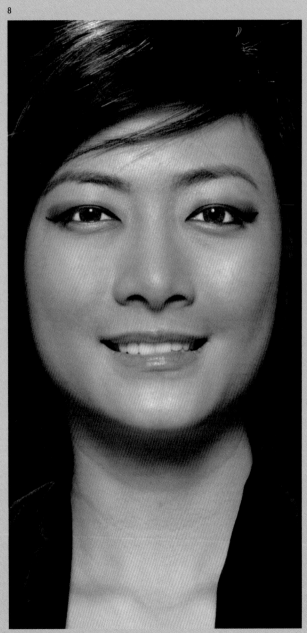

9

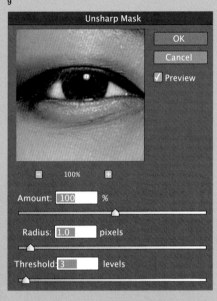

10

11

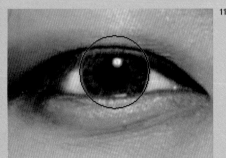

8: The best way to give an extra bit of life to eyes is to sharpen the pupils.

9: Bring up the Unsharp Mask dialog box by going to *Filter > Sharpen > Unsharp Mask*. Set Amount to 100%, Radius to 1.0, and Threshold to 3. Repeat this sharpening process two more times by going to *Filter > Unsharp Mask* (Ctrl/⌘ + F) twice.

10: At this stage the image will look over-sharpened. Open the History palette (*Window > History*) and you'll see the three Unsharp Mask history states. Select the Open state and then click the History Brush box next to the lowest Unsharp Mask history state.

11: Select the History Brush tool from the Toolbox. Zoom right into the first eye and adjust the brush so that it fits neatly over the pupil.

12: Just one click with the History Brush tool on each eye will be sufficient to sharpen the pupils and give them a little extra life. Compare the catchlights in the eyes here with those on the previous page.

Coloring eyes

Fashion photography, perhaps more than any other form of photography, makes good use of a number of image-editing techniques. We've already seen how easy it is to soften skin texture, and enhance teeth and eyes. Here we're going to take it one stage further and actually alter the color of the model's eyes. This process is often used to color coordinate a shoot.

← This model has beautiful hazel eyes, but the shoot may ask for another color. Begin by clicking the Quick Mask icon at the bottom of the Toolbox (or press Q).

↓ Zoom into one of the eyes, and with the Brush tool (press B), use a small, soft brush to paint over the existing pupils. You'll now have a mask over the eyes. To see the selection, press Q again, or the Quick Mask icon at the bottom of the Toolbox.

↓ You'll notice that everything but the eyes has been selected. To select the eyes, go to *Select > Inverse* (or press Shift + Ctrl/⌘ + I).

↓ Go to *Layer > New > Layer via Copy* (or press Ctrl/⌘ + J) to create a new layer that contains only the eyes. Name the layer "Eyes" for reference.

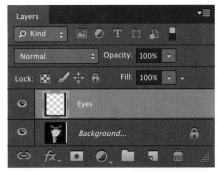

↑↗ With the Eyes layer selected, bring up the Color Balance dialog box (*Image > Adjustments > Color Balance*) and experiment with the various sliders until you have the color you want.

Traditionally, photographers used a variety of filters that they attached to the ends of their lenses in order to obtain various effects. One of the most common, and still used a lot today, is the gray grad filter. This is a filter that is gray at the top and gradually fades to clear (other shades are available), the idea

being that whenever it's difficult to balance the exposure between a bright sky and a dark landmass, the grad filter darkens the sky but leaves the land at the same light level. It's good practice to get this right in-camera whenever possible, however, here's a way of replicating the effect in software.

← A very common scenario. In order not to underexpose the foreground— made even harder thanks to the large area of shadow— the sky looks a little pale and washed out in this landscape.

Select the Gradient tool from the Toolbox, and in the Tool Options bar select the Foreground to Transparent gradient. Ensure that the Foreground color is set to black (press "D" for default).

← Create a new blank layer by clicking on the "Create a new layer" icon at the bottom of the Layers palette or press Shift + Ctrl/⌘ + N. With the Gradient tool, draw a vertical line from just outside the image area down to where the sky meets the horizon. Holding the Shift key will ensure you draw a straight line.

↓ When you let go of the Gradient tool, the sky will be overdrawn with a black gradient that fades to clear where you ended the line. Don't worry about the strength.

↓ Go to the Layers palette. With the gradient Filter layer selected, change the Blending Mode to Overlay. This will darken all the pixels where the Filter layer and Background layer meet. The effect may be quite strong.

↑ To fine tune the result, use the Opacity slider in the Layers palette. Here Opacity was set to 65%.

↑ Similar sky enhancement is achievable in Raw conversion software. Lightroom, for example, has a Graduated Filter (shown circled), which you can use on a selection to gradually increase (or decrease) exposure, contrast, saturation, and other settings.

Special Effects

Portrait photographers often use a soft-focus filter or even a soft-focus lens to soften portraits. This has the effect of smoothing skin and introducing a very gentle glow to the image, which tends to flatter the subject. The same effect can be achieved with an image-editing program, with greater control over the amount of soft focus you apply, as well as being able to eradicate it altogether in certain areas, such as the eyes and the mouth, which ideally you should keep as sharp as possible.

↑ Applying a soft-focus effect to this image will help to smooth the model's skin and give the image a lighter, gentler feel.

↑ Begin by copying the original Background image, by going to *Layer > Duplicate Layer...*, or press Ctrl/⌘ + J. Call the new layer Blur. In the Layers palette choose Lighten from the Blending Mode menu.

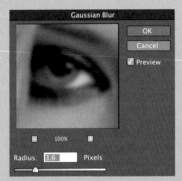

← With the Blur layer selected, go to *Filter > Blur > Gaussian Blur*. Dial in a sufficient amount of blur in the Radius box to soften the skin. You can see the effect in the main image. Click the Preview button on and off to gauge the effect of the Gaussian Blur filter.

↑ Now here's what you can't do using a filter on the camera. With the Blur layer active, click the "Add layer mask" icon at the bottom of the Layers palette. With a suitably sized soft brush (press B to bring up the Brush tool), paint with black as the foreground color over the subject's eyes and mouth. This will remove the soft-focus effect from these areas leaving the eyes and mouth sharp.

↑ Having re-introduced some sharpness back into the eyes and mouth, zoom out and click on and off the Blur layer's invisibility eye to see if you're happy with the result. You can tone down the soft-focus effect with the Opacity slider should you want. When you're satisfied with the new image, flatten it by going to *Layer > Flatten Image* and save (Ctrl/⌘ + S).

Misty landscape

Weather elements such as mist and fog can transform an otherwise typical and unextraordinary landscape scene into something dreamy, otherwordly, and truly worth photographing. Dedicated landscape photographers are often amateur meteorologists as well, keeping track of changes in the weather and seizing photogenic opportunities when they arise. Nevertheless, there is often an unavoidable amount of good luck involved in capturing exotic weather conditions—but certain aspects of mist and fog can be added digitally.

The primary effect of mist and fog in a landscape with a large amount of depth (distance between the foreground and background) is that objects are gradually obscured as you move farther away from the lens. This cumulative effect impact different parts of the frame to varying degrees, and so global adjustments to the entire scene are insufficient. Instead, we need to isolate certain elements of the scene and treat them differently—namely, leave most of the foreground elements unaffected, while incrementally obscuring the distant background.

↓ Here's the scene we're going to work on. The old bridge leads the eye nicely through the image to the distant hills beyond. These are already partially obscured by haze, but we want to increase this effect.

← First we need to isolate the foreground. Clicking on the Quick Mask icon at the bottom of the Toolbox allows the creation of a mask, which includes the old street lamp that is on the same focal plane as the rest of the foreground.

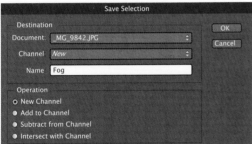

← With the mask complete go to *Select > Save Selection...* and give the selection a readily identifiable name. We've called ours Fog. We now have this selection available to call up later.

← The next step is to create the mist layer. Click on the Foreground Color box at the bottom of the Toolbox. This will bring up the Color Picker. Navigate the cursor to a medium gray area and click OK.

↑ Create a new blank layer either by clicking the "Create a new layer" icon at the bottom of the Layers palette or go to *Layer > New > Layer* (Shift + Ctrl/⌘ + N). Next, click on the Gradient tool (press G) and,

with the Foreground to Transparent gradient selected, draw a gradient from top to bottom of the image. In the Layers palette, change the new layer's Blending Mode to Screen.

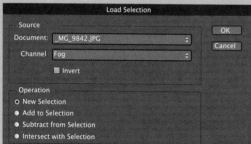

↑ With the Fog layer active, go to *Select > Load Selection* and choose Fog from the Channel pull-down menu. The mask will appear as a selection.

↑ Now return to the Layers palette, and still with the Fog layer selected, click the "Add layer mask" icon at the bottom of the Layers palette.

← As soon as you create the Layer Mask, the foreground should return to its original clarity.

← You can increase the atmospheric effect by duplicating the Fog layer (press Ctrl/⌘ + J) in the Layers palette.

← As we've seen, there is an increasing number of imaging tasks that can now be achieved in Raw conversion software —and black-and-white conversion is one of those too. As usual, the benefits are that you're making non-destructive changes, as well as utilizing the maximum amount of data when performing the task. This is particularly important in a monochrome conversion, as the more data you have at your disposal, the greater and more subtle are the tonal ranges you'll be able to extract from the image. Many Raw converters enable you to create black-and-white images; here Lightroom is used, which shares the same controls as Photoshop's Raw conversion software, ACR.

Despite the overwhelming popularity of color photography, driven primarily by glossy magazines featuring wonderfully saturated images, black-and-white photography still retains a large and influential following in certain circles. Many regard it as the pinnacle of photography—the only true art form of the medium.

Historically, photographers had to decide in advance whether they were going to create a color or a black-and-white image. Today, we have the luxury of shooting first and asking ourselves the color/black-and-white question later. Creating the optimum black-and-white print was an essential element of black-and-white photography, and a creative process in its own right. Today, making a black-and-white image remains a creative process and involves the same skills—an appreciation of and an understanding of tone—only the tools we now use offer us greater flexibility and experimentation. There are many ways to convert a color image to monochrome, some are more subtle and require greater input than others, but provide the best results—they're the ones we're going to cover over the next few pages.

1

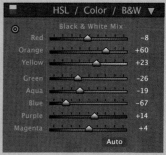

HSL / Color / **B&W** ▼	
Black & White Mix	
Red	−11
Orange	−21
Yellow	−25
Green	−28
Aqua	−17
Blue	+14
Purple	+19
Magenta	+5
	Auto

1: Navigate to the Grayscale tab in Lightroom. When you click on Grayscale, Lightroom will make a stab at doing the conversion for you.

The Auto result is quite good, with a nice range of tones, but there are one or two things that could be improved on.

2

HSL / Color / B&W ▼	
Black & White Mix	
Red	−8
Orange	+60
Yellow	+23
Green	−26
Aqua	−19
Blue	−67
Purple	+14
Magenta	+4
	Auto

3

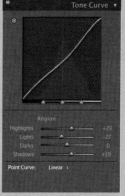

Tone Curve ▼	
Region	
Highlights	+29
Lights	−27
Darks	0
Shadows	+19
Point Curve:	Linear ⁝

2: Perhaps the first thing to notice in the Auto version is the lack of tonal difference between the blue wall and the off-white shutters: In the Auto image they could almost be the same color. By reducing the strength of the Blue filter the wall is rendered much darker—there is now a clear tonal distinction between the wall and the shutter. The other significant change is the bright yellow pot. In the Auto version, the pot appears quite dark. Increasing the Orange and Yellow filters makes the pot much lighter.

3: Finally, the Tone Curve was manipulated to reduce the contrast —with less dense shadows the image is easier to read.

The channel mixer conversion

Using the Channel Mixer for a black-and-white conversion has been a popular route to monochrome for some time. It allows you to control the proportions of each of the three color channels—red, green, and blue—in the black-and-white version. The process also benefits from using an adjustment layer, which allows you to change settings at any time.

RGB

Red channel

Green channel

Blue channel

Begin by assessing each of the color channels in turn. Ensure the "Show Channels in Color" box is not checked in the Interface preferences box (*Photoshop > Preferences > Interface*). The strength of this particular image lies in the shape of the house set against the blue sky. Looking at each channel in turn, it's clear that the Red channel provides the greatest contrast between the house and the sky, which emphasizes the shape of the house.

↑ To begin the conversion process create a Channel Mixer adjustment layer (*Layer > New Adjustment Layer > Channel Mixer...*) and click OK.

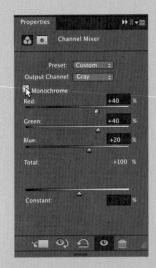

← In the resulting Channel Mixer Adjustment window, click the Monochrome box. Photoshop will automatically convert the image to black and white. More recent versions of the program also provide a number of preset filters found in the Channel Mixer pull-down menu. From our assessment earlier, we know that the Red channel provided the best contrast, so here we've selected Black & White with Red Filter (RGB).

↑ The preset filter worked well, but of course we can exaggerate the contrast even further by increasing the Red channel in the Channel Mixer dialog, as shown here. It's important to ensure the overall percentage remains as close to 100% as possible. As we've increased the Red it's necessary to reduce the Green and Blue accordingly. Also remember that adjustment layers come with their own layer mask should you want to isolate certain areas from the effect of the mask and bring back the color.

The so-called "Film and Filter" monochrome conversion method was developed by Russell Brown of Adobe. It utilizes two Hue/Saturation adjustment layers, one that converts the image to grayscale—the film—and another that affects the tonal qualities of the image in the same way colored filters on the end of a lens impact on monochrome images—the filter. Although extremely versatile, providing almost endless subtle tonal variations of a black-and-white image, this process is less intuitive than the Channel Mixer method covered earlier. However, with a bit of experimentation and trial and error, it's usually possible to arrive at a satisfactory result.

↑ To begin the "film and filter" conversion method create a new Hue/Saturation adjustment layer (*Layer > New Adjustment Layer > Hue/Saturation...*).

Set Saturation to -100 by moving the slider all the way to the left. This layer represents the black-and-white film, so call it "Film."

→ Click on the Background layer and make sure it's selected, then create another Hue/Saturation adjustment layer. This layer represents the effects of using different colored filters over the lens. Change its blending mode to Color and call it Filter.

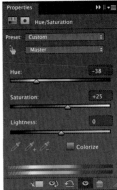

← With the "Filter" layer active, experiment with the Hue slider to see the effect it has. Here, although the conversion is true to the original color version, it looks dark and the dark lettering on the T-shirt is difficult to read.

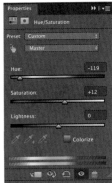

← Adjust the color of the filter by sliding the Hue slider. In this version the T-shirt is much lighter (as are the skin tones), making the dark lettering easier to read. Flatten the image (*Layer > Flatten Image*) to keep the finished file size down.

Black & white adjustment layer

Photoshop's latest version of the Black and White adjustment layer has a powerful new feature. It enables you to stroke the cursor to adjust the brightness of areas of related tones. This makes the entire creative process of fine tuning black-and- white conversions much more intuitive, as you're working on the image itself rather than via a series of sliders, which for some people don't easily relate to the image. Let's look at a specific example to see how this works.

1

2

1: We are going to apply a Black & White adjustment layer to this atmospheric shot of a solitary tree.

2: Go to *Layer > New Adjustment Layer > Black & White...* As soon as you click OK to the new layer, Photoshop instantly displays a black-and- white version of the original image. Photoshop makes a commendable effort at the conversion, but what if we wanted to darken the sky and lighten the grass?

3: Looking at the Black & White adjustment dialog shows the usual color sliders, which we could use to adjust the brightness of the various tones in the image.

3

Properties

Black & White

Preset: Default

Tint   Auto

Reds: 40

Yellows: 60

Greens: 40

Cyans: 60

Blues: 20

Magentas: 80

4: However, this time we're going to eschew the sliders and click on the hand icon at the top left of the adjustment window. To darken the sky, we simply click on the sky and drag the cursor to the left. Photoshop samples the pixels at the point you click the mouse. When you drag the pointer left, all the pixels of a similar color range in the image are darkened (moving right would brighten them).

5: To lighten the grass, simply stroke the cursor to the right. Again all pixels of a similar color will be made lighter. Looking at the adjustment window having completed the edit shows the Cyans slider way off to the left and the Yellows slider to the right. Clicking on the Tint box allows you to tint the image with a color of your choice.

4

5

Duotones & tritones

Traditionally, duotones are monochrome images with a small amount of color added. They were commonly seen in "fine art" photography books. During the printing process, a second (and third in the case of tritones) color is used—usually a dark brown or another form of "warm black"—to increase the tonal rendition and range of the print. The process was often a hit or miss affair, and required a great deal of experience on the part of the printer. With image-editing software you can experiment with a variety of tones before committing to the finished print.

← To create a duotone in Photoshop, you need to start with a grayscale image (click *Image > Mode > Grayscale*). You'll be asked if you want to discard the color information in the image. Click OK. Now go to *Image > Mode > Duotone* to bring up the Duotone Options dialog box. There are numerous options in the Preset pull-down menu worth trying. Alternatively you can click on the second color box to bring up the Color Picker and select a color of your choice.

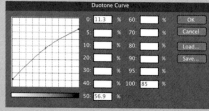

← Clicking on the small curves window brings up that color's Duotone Curve. Here you can manipulate the curve to affect the tonal distribution of the second color. Click OK when you're happy. To print the image you need to go to *Image > Mode > RGB Color* and save the file.

← To add a third color, simply choose Tritone from the Type pull-down menu. Again there is a large number of Presets to choose from, which utilize printer-recognized PANTONE colors (as do the duotone presets). Alternatively you can choose your own colors.

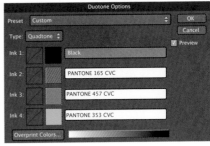

← Finally, it's even possible to create a quadtone, which uses four different tones. The same process as creating a duotone or tritone applies.

4.08   **Split toning Raw images**

In earlier versions of Photoshop, the only way to create duotones was to use the Duotone command, but in more recent versions of the program, and also with Lightroom and Aperture, it's possible to

apply split toning to a Raw file. Again the benefits of this are that the entire process is non-destructive, and you'll be able to utilize the maximum amount of data when creating the image.

↓ Begin by converting your color image to a grayscale one. Navigate to the HSL/Color/B&W panel in Lightroom, and click

on B&W. Next, use the various color sliders to create a black-and-white version of the image that you're happy with.

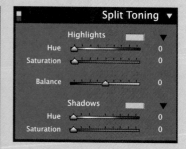

↑ When you're happy with the grayscale image, click on the Split Toning tab.

↓ The Split Toning dialog box is straightforward and intuitive. Start by selecting a color for the highlights—here we've chosen a cold blue—and set an appropriate saturation level. As is often the case, less is more when it comes to the Saturation slider.

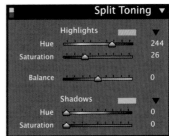

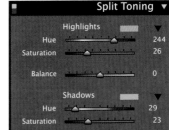

← When you've selected the highlight tone, it's time to move on to the shadows. Here we've introduced a warm, sepia color to offset the cold blue. You can, of course, go back to the Highlights controls to fine tune the tone. In addition you can use the Balance slider to subtly place greater emphasis on either the shadows or highlights.

One of the most enduring and popular types of toned image is the sepia print. The warm browns powerfully evoke a bygone era. Achieving consistent results conventionally in the darkroom was no mean feat. The chemicals used were easily affected by temperature, and even a slight deviation from the set time would produce wildly varying results. Today, in the digital darkroom, we don't have to endure any of these sensitive variables. There are numerous ways of recreating a sepia-toned effect, but the one described here can be achieved with just about any image-editing software; in addition it's quick, very easy, and as effective as far more complicated versions.

↑ This photograph was taken at a local steam fair, and provides a perfect subject for a sepia effect.

↑ Call up a Hue/Saturation adjustment layer (*Layer > New Adjustment Layer > Hue/Saturation*, and click OK). Click the Colorize box in the adjustments window. Try various combinations of Hue and Saturation slider settings until you've got the sepia color you want. You could now save the image, by going to *Layer > Flatten Image* and saving.

← We've taken the image to another stage here by reducing the overall brightness using Levels and introducing a grain effect (*Filter > Noise > Add Noise...*)

Cyanotypes

Although the cyanotype process was invented by the English astronomer John Herschel in 1842 as a means of reproducing his handwritten notes, the process was first used as a photographic medium by Anna Atkins, in a series of books illustrating ferns and plants. A cyanotype's typical blue color (hence the name) is the result of mixing ferrous salts with potassium ferricyanide, which combine to form a mixture known as Prussian blue. Traditionally, sunlight was used to make the exposure, and the resulting print was then "developed" using running water. The soluble salts dissolve in the water leaving the insoluble Prussian blue forming the image.

↑ You need to start with an image that contains only black and white. Here the Threshold command was applied (*Image > Adjustments > Threshold...*), with a value of around 120 to ensure detail remained in the church tower.

↓ Click on the "Set foreground color" box in the Toolbox to bring up the Color Picker. Choose an appropriate blue color. Return to the image and select all the black areas with the Magic Wand tool. Go to *Edit > Fill* and set the Use option to Foreground Color, and set the Blending Mode to Lighter Color and Opacity to around 50%.

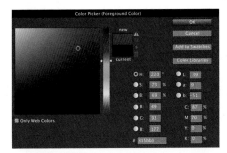

→ Applying the blue color creates a reasonable cyanotype-like result. But we can improve on this slightly.

1

Canvas Size	
Current Size: 23.4M	OK
Width: 82.41cm	Cancel
Height: 123.61cm	

New Size: 33.7M

Width: 120 percent
Height: 120 percent
☐ Relative
Anchor:

Canvas extension color: Background

3

Size: 150 px

Hardness: 0%

25 50

Add Noise 4

OK
Cancel
☑ Preview

25%

Amount: 50 %

Distribution
◉ Uniform
○ Gaussian

☑ Monochromatic

2

1: Go to *Image > Canvas Size...* and increase the overall size of the canvas so that you give the image a large white border. Here we've increased the canvas by 120% all round.

2: With the Rectangular Marquee tool draw around the image. Go to *Select > Inverse* to select the white border.

3: Select the Brush tool (press B) and start painting around the outside of the image. You're trying to replicate the original application of the chemicals to the paper before the large-format negative is placed over the paper. Vary the brush size and type, and build up "layers" of color.

4: When you're happy with the fake border, go to *Select > Inverse* again. This time the main image will be selected. Go to *Filter > Noise > Add Noise...* and introduce some grain to break up the flat color of the main image a little.

5: Finally go to *Layer > Flatten Image* to make the file ready for output.

Solarization / Sabattier effect

Solarization is the reversal of certain tones in a print following a deliberate secondary exposure while the print is being processed. It is closely associated with the Sabattier Effect, but strictly the latter refers to overexposure of negative film. However, both are concerned with the effect of tone reversal and that is what we'll be doing in this project. Photoshop has a Solarize filter, however, it offers no level of adjustment, and to that end results are usually hit or miss. You'll gain far more control using a Curves adjustment layer and experimenting with a variety of tonal inversions. You'll also have the benefit of trying out alternative blending modes and setting the opacity.

↑ Although it's possible to apply this solarization effect to a color image, the results are difficult to predict, and traditionally the effect was commonly applied to black-and-white images. This photo was converted to monochrome using the Black & White command.

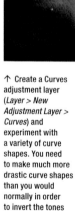 ↑ Create a Curves adjustment layer (*Layer > New Adjustment Layer > Curves*) and experiment with a variety of curve shapes. You need to make much more drastic curve shapes than you would normally in order to invert the tones in the image.

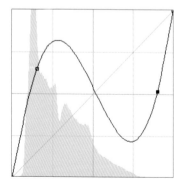

↑ For this image a steep U-shaped curve provided the most pleasing result.

↑ Further experimentation involved trying out various blending modes. Here Pin Light helped to increase the Solarization effect. This was controlled by reducing the opacity of the Curves adjustment layer. With the Curves adjustment layer's mask active, part of the face was painted over in black to bring back a little of the original background layer. Finally, a very light blue tone was introduced using Variations.

Posterization

Posterization is the process of grouping together a continuous range of tones into a small, distinct number of flat tones. The result is a very stylized, graphic image. The technique has been used to create posters (hence the name) for many years. The success of the process relies on choosing a suitable photo— distinctive shapes and blocks of color usually work best—but even then the results can be very difficult to predict. That's why the most productive means to work is using adjustment layers, which you can continually return to and amend, until you arrive at a result that works for you.

↓ This image has good blocks of color and easily identifiable shapes, so the posterization should work well. As with the solarization technique, it's possible to posterize a color image, but as each color channel will have a minimum of two levels, this restricts you to an overall minimum of six levels, which may be too many— making the image difficult to read.

← Convert the color image to grayscale using a Channel Mixer adjustment layer. Click the OK prompt after going to *Layer > New Adjustment Layer > Channel Mixer...*, and then check the Monochrome box in the Channel Mixer window. Adjust the channel sliders to optimize the image so that there are clear differences in tone in key areas of the image. Remember, you're not trying to create a finished grayscale image, so how it looks at this stage is unimportant. You don't even have to aim for a channel total of 100%.

↑ Next go to *Layer > New Adjustment Layer > Posterize....* Again, click OK when prompted. You then need to set the number of Levels.

The default is four, and this usually provides good results. Being an adjustment layer, however, you can always revisit this later.

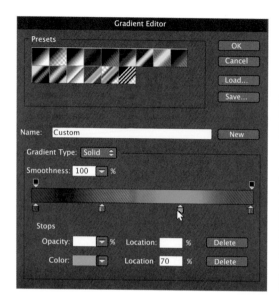

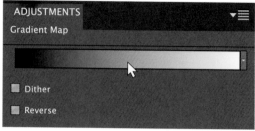

↑ To add color go to *Layer > New Adjustment Layer > Gradient Map...* to bring up the Gradient Map. Then click on the gradient bar to bring up the Gradient Editor. Starting with a standard grayscale map, click on the bottom of the grayscale map to add a new color stop. Double-clicking in the small box at the bottom of the color stop will bring up the Color Picker, from which you can select your colors.

← Moving the stops along the gradient will affect which color is applied to which tone. It's worth experimenting with moving the stops as this will have dramatic impact on the image.

New Gradient...

Rename Gradient...
Delete Gradient

Text Only
✓ Small Thumbnail
Large Thumbnail
Small List
Large List

Preset Manager...

Reset Gradients...
Load Gradients...
Save Gradients...
Replace Gradients...

Color Harmonies 1
Color Harmonies 2
Metals
Noise Samples
Pastels
Simple
Special Effects
Spectrums

↑ There is also a vast number of preset colors to choose from. Here, the Color Harmonies 1 gradient selection was loaded, and an example chosen from there. The opacity of the Gradient Map adjustment layer was also reduced to tone down the colors.

→ As the entire project has been set up with adjustment layers, it pays to return to each experiment with the various settings. In this example, the number of Levels was increased to six.

Cross-processing

Cross-processing was a technique first discovered in the 1960s, but made popular in the 1980s and early 1990s, particularly in the genre of fashion photography. The technique involved using developing chemicals intended for different film stock—and it seems likely that early examples of cross-processing were unintentional. As is often the case with erroneous wet processing techniques, results were based very much on trial and error. With image-editing software, however, it's possible to take control of the entire process so that you achieve the desired result every time.

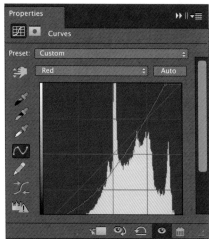

↑ A Japanese model dressed in a fancy dress costume with colored contact lenses makes for a good cross-processing subject.

↑ The majority of the effect is achieved using a Curves adjustment layer (*Layer > New Adjustment Layer > Curves...*). Start with the Red channel. Reds usually become more contrasting in cross-processed images, so move the shadow region of the curve (bottom left) down to darken the red shadows and move the top right point to the left to brighten red highlights.

↓ Next, switch to the blue channel. Cross-processed blues tend to lack contrast, so move the bottom left point up and the top right down to flatten the blue tones.

↓↓ Like reds, greens need to be more contrasting, so in the Green channel create a gentle S-shaped curve to increase the contrast.

↓ The image is now close to the cross-processed look. The off-whites, deeper red of the collar, and the greenish background are all reminiscent of the effect. But we're not quite finished yet.

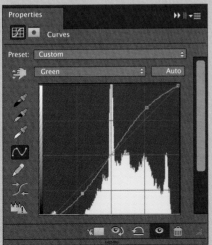

↓ Although we've increased the contrast quite drastically in two of the three color channels, we need to increase the overall contrast in the image as well. Create another Curves adjustment layer, set its blending mode to Luminosity so only the tones in the image are affected and not the colors. With RGB selected, set a gentle S-curve to increase overall contrast.

↓ Just increasing the contrast a little has provided the gritty look you get with cross-processed images. It has also resulted in blown highlights, which are most apparent in the gloves. Blown highlights are a common feature of cross-processed photos, and add to the authenticity. This image could be ready to go.

↓ However, if you want to control the level of blown highlights and tone down the contrast a little, select the first Curves adjustment layer and change the blending mode to Color. This has the effect of ensuring that only the hue and saturation values are adjusted for each of the channel curve amendments we made earlier.

↓ The Color blending mode change has fixed the worst offending blown highlights and softened the contrast a little; a cross-processed look, but with the subtle control only available with image-editing software. You can of course reduce the whole effect by reducing the Opacity of both Curves adjustment layers. Flatten the image (*Layer > Flatten Image*) when you've got the look you want.

Hand-tinting

Hand-tinting monochrome images has been around for nearly as long as monochrome plates themselves. In the 1840s the only way to obtain a color photograph was to apply colored paints or adhesive powder to Daguerreotypes—an early type of photograph. This work was often carried out by skilled artists who also specialized in miniature portraits. The intention was not to apply a thick layer of color in order to recreate a realistic impression, but merely to add a subtle wash. Although, as usual, there are a number of ways of recreating the hand-tinted look, many simply rely on using a duplicate monochrome layer, subtly revealing the color from the layer beneath. This is quick and effective, but half the fun of hand-tinting is choosing your own colors. The method described here requires some patience, but provides more authentic-looking results.

↑ Start with a black-and-white image (using a monochrome conversion of your choice if necessary). Create a new blank layer (*Layer > New > Layer*) and change its blending mode to Color; name it color.

↑ Now it's simply a case of using the brush tool (press B) at various sizes (use the "[" and "]" keys to change size), to paint over the background layer. Click the Foreground Color box in the Toolbox to bring up the Color Picker. The painting doesn't have to be precise—remember you're simply creating a color wash.

← When you've finished coloring over the monochrome image, reduce the opacity of the Color layer. Sit back and admire your work.

A good way to reinforce the color wash aspect of the original hand-tinting process is to blur the Color layer. This helps to merge opposing colors, but does reduce color saturation. Either increase the Color layer's opacity or use the Hue/Saturation command to boost the color a little. Don't forget to flatten your image *Layer > Flatten Image* when you're done.

Digital infrared photography is becoming increasingly popular, and absolutely remarkable results can be achieved. For a true infrared image you need either to place a deep red filter (Hoya R72) over the camera's lens, or get your old digital SLR converted for infrared. The benefits of the latter route include much faster shutter speeds and being able to freely change lenses. Traditionally, infrared images were primarily black and white, but more recent exponents are using image-editing techniques to colorize their infrared photos. The images here are not infrared, but any photo is two layers away from an infrared look.

← Images with green trees, grass, and bright blue sky are usually the most effective for an infrared make-over. This is true in the real infrared world.

← To increase the tonal difference between the various colors in this image, color saturation was increased using the Saturation slider in the Hue/Saturation command.

↑ Duplicate the background layer (*Layer > Duplicate Layer...*, or press Ctrl/⌘ + J). Make a negative version of this new layer by going to *Image > Adjustments > Invert* (or press Ctrl/⌘ + I). Duplicate this inverted layer, but invert it back to a positive image, so that it is a duplicate of the background. On screen, you'll be back where you started. However, change the Invert 2 layer's blending mode to Luminosity and you'll have an instant faux infrared image.

← When you've created the infrared image, flatten it (*Layer > Flatten Image*). You can now reduce the color saturation for a more subtle result.

← Alternatively, you can adjust the Hue slider in the Hue/Saturation dialog and change the colors of the entire image.

HDR, or High Dynamic Range images, in which a series of progressively exposed shots of the same scene are combined to make one image with a complete tonal range from highlights to shadows, have been around for many years in analog photography. Now, however, with the advent of affordable digital cameras and image-editing programs the process is more popular than ever.

And to help, there is software that will combine the images for you and create a single HDR image, which can then be tonemapped (a form of very localized contrast control) to recreate an image that displays the entire dynamic range. In this section we will look at a couple of ways you can create your own HDR images. Results vary from the naturalistic to the highly stylized.

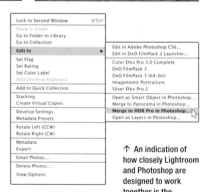

↑ This landscape was shot without the aid of a graduated filter to hold the highlights in the sky. Instead the photographer shot a series of five bracketed photos (of which three are shown above) so that between the five shots the complete dynamic range of the scene, from the brightest highlights to the darkest shadows, was captured.

→ In Photoshop begin the HDR process with *Automate > Merge to HDR...* It's recommended that when shooting a sequence for HDR that you use the Raw format as, being 12- or 14-bit files, these will give you the greatest possible tonal information.

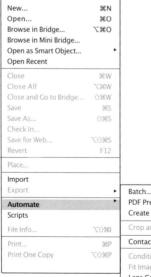

↑ An indication of how closely Lightroom and Photoshop are designed to work together is the fact that you can export a bracketed sequence directly from Lightroom to Photoshop's Merge to HDR Pro feature.

→ Having selected *Automate > Merge to HDR...* navigate to the source sequence. If you've shot the sequence handheld using continuous shooting mode, click the *Attempt to Automatically Align Source Images* box. This will usually successfully correct any misalignment issues between frames due to slight camera movement. Next click *OK*.

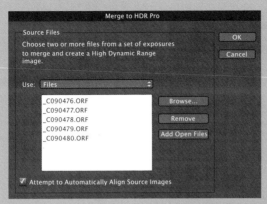

↓ The Merge to HDR Pro window shows a default preview of the tonemapped image, along with the source images beneath it. To the right are the various controls and sliders (*see page 132*). One important option to note is the *Remove Ghosts* box. Tick this if the sequence comprised any moving objects such as swaying branches, waves, or even people and cars. This will appear misaligned or "ghosted" as they move between shots. Photoshop will use a single frame from the sequence wherever it detects ghosting artifacts.

→ Aside from the *Preset* settings, which we'll come to in a bit, Merge to HDR Pro also features three key panels, all of which fit into the *Mode* pane. True HDR images are 32-bits and cannot be accurately rendered on a computer monitor. To work on the image you'll need to set Mode to 16-bit. Photoshop has four conversion options available in the Mode pull-down menu. Experiment with each to see how they work, but the one that offers the most control is Local Adaptation. As its name suggests this option allows you to adjust brightness and contrast at local regions over the image. Edge Glow Radius determines the size of the local regions, while Strength determines the tonal range at which pixels are included in one region or another. In the Tone and Detail pane, a Gamma setting of 1.0 provides maximum dynamic range, while higher settings increase contrast and lower settings emphasize midtones. The Exposure slider sets brightness, and Detail sets sharpness.

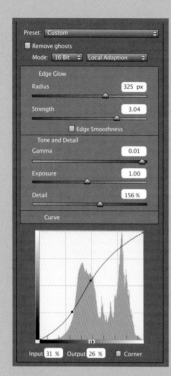

← Despite offering a number of presets, few of the Merge to HDR Pro settings work particularly well without a fair amount of additional manual intervention. They may provide you with a starting point, but they don't offer one-click results. Below is the Surrealistic setting using the five source images shown earlier.

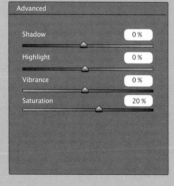

← The Curve pane provides the familiar Curve control that allows you to adjust and set tones and contrast. The Advanced pane provides sliders to set brightness for Shadow and Highlight regions, as well as offering Vibrance and Saturation color controls.

↓ Although it's possible to get acceptable results using Photoshop's Merge to HDR Pro feature, the controls aren't intuitive–new users may find a good deal of trial and error is needed to arrive at usable results.

If you don't own Photoshop, but are keen to experiment with some tonemapped HDR imagery, one of the best and most popular HDR programs available is Photomatix Pro. Photomatix has been around since digital HDR first became popular, and the software has developed and evolved over time. Available either as a standalone program or as a plug-in for Lightroom, Aperture, and Photoshop, Photomatix has a comprehensive tool set and is very capable of creating a range of HDR styles, from the photorealistic to the hyperrealistic.

↑↗→ The three exposure-bracketed shots of this World War II jeep, shown here, cover the dynamic range of the scene.

← Having imported the sequence into Lightroom, it's possible to then select them all and export directly from Lightroom to Photomatix Pro, either via *File > Export* with *Preset > Photomatix Pro...* or by right-clcking and selecting *Export > Photomatix Pro...*

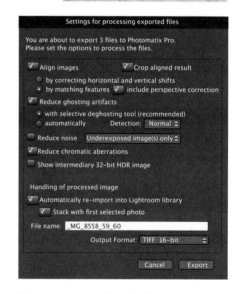

↑ Before Photomatix creates the full 32-bit HDR image, you're presented with a preprocessing screen that offers a number of important options. Like Photoshop's Merge to HDR Pro the two most important options are concerned with aligning the source images and deghosting.

→ Photomatix's deghosting routine is one of the most successful out of all the HDR software available. Although there's a fully automatic option, the semimanual process is recommended as this ensures deghosting only occurs specifically in the areas you want. In this example the fluttering of the flag has been captured across the three frames resulting in the ghosting effect. To fix this simply select the ghosted area(s) and click Preview Deghosting. Here the ghosted flag is rendered as a single, clearly defined item. When you're satisfied with the deghosting, click OK.

Process: ● Tone Mapping
○ Exposure Fusion

Method: Details Enhancer ⌃

Strength — 100

Color Saturation — 50

Luminosity — +6.0

Detail Contrast — +6.0

Lightning Adjustments — Medium

Natural | Surreal

☑ Lighting Effects — Natural+ | Surreal+

▼ Hide More Options

Smooth Highlights — 0

White Point — 0.500%

Black Point — 0.010%

Gamma — 1.00

Temperature — 0

▼ Hide Advanced Options

Micro–smoothing — 3.0

Saturation Highlights — 0

Saturation Shadows — 0

Shadows Smoothness — 0

Shadows Clipping — 0

☐ 360° image

→ Even if the various presets don't provide you with a result you're immediately happy with, they usually provide a good starting point.

← Although for the uninitiated Photomatix's main control panel looks complicated, the sliders are relatively quick to master. It's worth noting that as well as two tone mapping methods, Photomatix Pro also offers an Exposure Fusion option. This setting doesn't utilize a tone mapping algorithm, it simply blends the highlights with the shadows from the various source images depending on the user settings. The lack of any localized processing can yield very clean looking, artifact-free images, providing naturalistic results. But if you want something a little more painterly or surreal select the Tone Mapping option. The default option is

Details Enhancer, which offers more control than the alternative Tone Compressor.

Strength acts like a master control over local contrast and detail settings. A low setting ensures any other adjustments are minimal. To have any real impact use a Strength setting of between 70 and 100.

Color Saturation is self-explanatory and works like the Saturation slider in Photoshop.

Luminosity sets tonal compression. Move the slider to the right to brighten shadows. Detail Contrast sets how much contrast is applied to details. Moving the slider to the right will darken the image.

Lighting Adjustments determines how local contrast and brightness is applied. Moving the slider to the left creates a more surreal effect, while to the right more naturalistic results are possible. If you click Lighting Effects you'll get some presets to experiment with.

More Options and Advanced Options both provide ways of making fine adjustments to the image.

Smooth Highlights is helpful at reducing gray skies that are a common feature of tone-mapped images.

White Point and Black Point settings determine maximum and minimum brightness values

of the tone-mapped image respectively, while the Gamma control sets mid-tone brightness.

Temperature adjusts the color temperature of the image: Left for a blue, cool look, right for a redder, warmer look.

Micro-smoothing can reduce noise in smooth flat areas such as skies. The remaining sliders set color saturation in highlights and shadows, while Shadow Smoothness reduces localized contrast enhancement in shadow regions.

Shadows Clipping darkens shadows and is used to disguise noise.

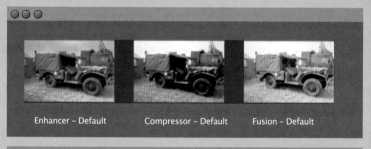

Enhancer – Default   Compressor – Default   Fusion – Default

Enhancer – Grunge   Enhancer – Smooth   Enhancer – B&W

Built-In | My Presets

→ These images show how adept Photomatix is at various HDR tone mapping styles—naturalistic at top and surrealistic below. Once you've got a tone mapped preview that fits the type of HDR image you want to create, import the 16-bit TIFF back into Lightroom, Aperture, or Photoshop and make your final post-production adjustments there. You'll find that sharpening for output is usually required to tease out any final detail in the image.

Panoramas

Before the advent of digital photography, creating a panoramic image was usually a complicated and expensive business, often requiring specialist equipment, such as rotating cameras. The easiest way was to crop a long narrow section, but this often resulted in poor print quality. Today, thanks primarily to incredibly sophisticated stitching software, creating panoramas is quick and easy, and the results usually far exceed anything that was achievable during the days of film.

These are the three images that will be combined to make a panorama. In the early days of stitching software, it helped to take the images using a tripod and carefully aligning your images when they overlapped. Modern software is so good at recognizing similar areas in an image—even if they aren't aligned across two or more images—that you can now safely shoot panoramas just by hand-holding the camera and roughly overlapping the frames. One good tip, however, is to shoot in Manual mode so the camera doesn't automatically adjust the exposure, leading to slight variations in tone that will become apparent when the images are stitched together.

↓ After cropping the image, go to *Layer > Flatten Image*. You can now make overall adjustments to the panorama, such as Levels, Curves, Hue/ Saturation, and so on, before saving the file.

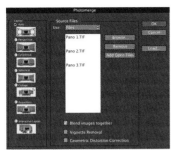

← Go to *Automate > Photomerge...* to start, then navigate to the images that will make up the panorama. There are various Layout options visible down the left-hand side of the screen, but selecting Auto works best if you want a standard panorama. Ensure Blend Images Together is checked at the bottom of the window, and click OK.

↓ Photoshop will take a few moments to stitch the images together, but you shouldn't have to wait too long before the preview panorama appears. At this stage you won't be able to do much to the image, other than crop it so that you have a panorama with clean edges.

Although you're unlikely to want to add text to your images too often, it's useful to learn how it's done. Most image-editing programs have a staggering number of text styles and effects you can apply to text, making it quite an entertaining process. There may well be special occasions such as birthdays, anniversaries, or religious holidays, when adding some text to an appropriate image as a greeting card makes a very personal and much-appreciated gesture.

← This photo of a rising sun captured in the tail of a airplane waiting on the runway is graphically simple, with plenty of area to text. It can even be divided into three distinct horizontal sections for three separate text treatments, if desired.

← To begin, select the Type tool from the Toolbox. Photoshop has both a Horizontal Type tool and a Vertical Type tool, and here we're going to use the Horizontal tool. Place the cursor roughly where you want the type to be. Type the wording you're going to use. (In this case, it's a band name, to go on a concert poster.) You can move this later so it doesn't have to be in exactly the right place, and the default font will probably not be set in stone—you have plenty of opportunity to experiment with your font choices.

← When you've finished typing, click the confirmation tick in the Tool Options bar to approve the type. Go to the Layers palette and you'll see a new text layer with your wording will have been generated automatically.

↓ Highlight the wording with the Type tool and choose a typeface from the Tool Options bar. Photoshop has dozens to choose from. Next, click on the color square in the Tool Options bar to bring up the Color Picker. Choose a color you like. You can also choose from a selection of warped text styles.

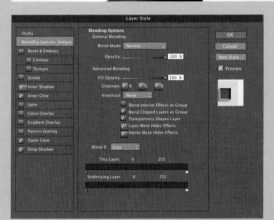

← With the Move tool selected, and ensuring that the Show Transform Controls box is checked in the Tool Options bar, you can stretch, lengthen, and move your type into its final position.

← Next comes the really fun part. With the text layer selected, click on the "Add a layer style" box at the bottom of the Layers palette. This will bring up a list of effects that you can apply to the text. Clicking any one of them brings up the main Layer Style dialog window.

Here you can add a drop shadow (setting its size, distance, and so on), an inner shadow, inner glow—in fact just about every text embellishment you can think of.

↓ Once you've finished adding the various text styles you want, flatten the image (*Layer > Flatten Image*) and you're ready to go.

Thursday 21 December
The Old Market
Doors @ 9PM

Creating montages

Combining a number of images together to create a montage in most image-editing software is a straightforward task—the hardest part is finding the right sort of images, and having the artistic vision to know what you want to do with them. A photomontage can be a very powerful artistic expression, or used in a more straightforward fashion to simply create an image that can be placed in a photo album or shown to family and friends—that's the intention here.

← Begin by choosing an appropriate background image, one that will form a good base on which to place other images.

← Open the next image you wish to place in the montage. Select the entire image (*Select > All*) and copy it (*Edit > Copy*). Go to the first image you opened and paste the second (*Edit > Paste*). With the Move tool selected, and ensuring that the Show Transform Controls box is ticked in the Tool Options bar, hold the Shift key (to retain the image's proportions) and reduce the second image by dragging inward on one of the corner handles. Click in the image to place it roughly where you want the image to be in the final montage.

← In the Layers palette you should now have a second layer—your second image. Double-click on the Layer 1 text and rename the layer with a readily identifiable label (in this case "Church"). Repeat with another image. Now create a layer mask (byclicking the "Add layer mask" icon at the bottom of the Layers palette).

← With the layer mask active, select the Brush tool (press B) and set a low opacity in the Tool Options bar. With an appropriately sized brush, start to paint out the selected image. The idea is to blend the image into the background.

←↑ Build up the montage by copying and pasting new images onto your original background image. Use layer masks to paint around the edges so they blend smoothly into the background image. Also try experimenting with various blending modes and the opacity slider to vary the look. Soft Light is particularly good at blending two images together.

Styles

Blending Options: Default

☐ Bevel & Emboss

☐ Contour

☐ Texture

☑ Stroke

☐ Inner Shadow

☐ Inner Glow

☐ Satin

← Our holiday montage is almost complete. To finish off, we're going to add some text. Click on the Horizontal Type tool and place your text as described earlier. Choose some appropriate text styles by clicking on the "Add a layer style" box at the bottom of the Layers palette.

↓ Before flattening the image, check the position of each element—remember you need to click the appropriate layer in the Layers palette to adjust it. Once you're done, flatten the image (*Layer > Flatten Image*) and you're now ready to print or send the image via email.

High-key portrait

High-key images are made up of large areas of very bright tones, with few intermediate or dark tones to provide detail and offer some tonal balance. Although a high-key treatment can be used with any genre of photography, it's particularly popular in fashion and portrait photography, where the bright, almost overexposed tones act to soften skin, particularly of lighter-skinned models. As well as the softening effect, which helps to hide any skin blemishes, high-key portraits also tend to flatten facial features, and create a light, delicate atmosphere.

← This image is evenly lit, with no visible shadows on the model's face. Her green top and delicate skin tones, makes this portrait an ideal candidate for a quick high-key treatment.

↑ Go to *Layer > Duplicate Layer...* to copy the background layer, or press Ctrl/⌘ + J. Call the new layer "High Key." With the High Key layer active, change the blending mode to Screen. Instantly the entire image should brighten considerably in tone.

↓ To brighten the tones even further, duplicate the High Key layer. Here we've reduced the overall effect by reducing the second High Key layer's opacity.

Creating a layer mask and painting with black over the eyes, mouth, and other key areas keeps these features from becoming too pale.

↓ High-key portraits can be particularly effective in black and white. This version was created using the Black & White command.

Mimicking tilt-shift effects

This is one of the oldest photographic effects—authentically brought on by the tilt and shift movements of large-format lens bellow, but recently enjoying a resurgence in popularity due to its widespread use in mobile imaging. Essentially, by blurring out selective areas at the top and bottom of the frame, you can create a miniaturization effect that accentuates the area in focus. It works because this particularly shallow depth of field usually only occurs at macro focusing distances, so your brain interprets the scene as being an extreme close-up of correspondingly miniscule subjects.

← It's best to work with an image that has plenty of depth to it, with objects stretching from foreground to the horizon line. Including objects of known size also reinforces the effect—everyone knows the size of a human body or car, and can compare what they see against their expectation.

↑ Go to *Filter > Blur > Tilt-Shift*, which overlays four lines and a center circle on the image. Position the center circle over the main object of interest, pull the other lines to define the areas in focus and blurred, and adjust the amount of blur by dragging around the center circle.

→ The finishing touch was a slight crop at the bottom, to pull the attention forward and cut out the blank area at the bottom of the frame. The resulting image has four human figures and the front of a bus in sharp focus, but rendered as tiny figurines set amidst a dense urban landscape.

Tip

It helps to apply tilt-shift effects to images that were shot from above, looking down on the main subject. That is the expected orientation in many macro shots, and thus has the strongest impression on the viewer. It doesn't have to be a steep view down, however—an angle between 15–45 degrees is ideal.

Adding borders

Adding a complementary border to a print can be an excellent way to show off your work in its best light. Borders can take the form of simple black or white edging, or be more creative using some of Photoshop's Filters. Much, of course, depends on the print around which you're placing the border, and the final effect you want to achieve. In addition, there are a number of websites that provide ready-made "art" borders for a really unique look.

← For a simple frame, open the image around which you want to place the border. Go to *Image > Canvas Size*. Increase the width and height of the image by the size you want your border to be. Here we wanted the border to be 2 cm, so the width and height were increased by 2 cm. Next, select the color of your border. We've chosen black, but it can be any color you like. Clicking on the color square at the bottom of the Canvas Size dialog window will open the Color Picker. Click OK.

↑ The finished picture with its new border is ready in a matter of seconds.

↓ You can use Photoshop's brushes to make more inventive borders. Open the image you want to add the border to. In the Layers palette, double-click the background layer and click OK. You'll now be able to add a layer mask.

→ Go to the main image and draw a rectangular border with the Marquee tool. Invert the selection to create the border. With the layer mask active in the Layers palette, go to *Edit > Fill* and fill the border with white.

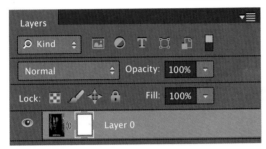

↑ With the Eraser selected (press E). In the Tool Options bar choose a brush that provides plenty of texture. We've used number 63 from the Dry Media Brushes

selection. Paint with white over the layer mask to delete the edges of the image. Paint black to replace the image. The idea is to end up with a richly textured edge.

→ Flatten the image when you've got the edge you want. Here we've also added a black border.

↑ Photoshop's Filters can also be used to make borders. Open the image and with the Rectangular Marquee tool, draw a rectangle inside the edge of the image. The thickness of the border determines the thickness of the frame.

↑ Go to *Select > Inverse* and then press Edit in Quick Mask Mode at the bottom of the Toolbox (or press Q). You now have a mask where the border won't take effect. Apply a small amount of Gaussian Blur to the mask. The greater the blur amount, the more the border will intrude into the image.

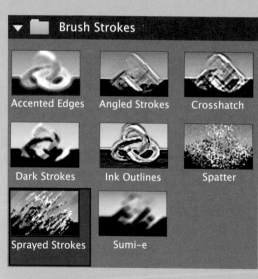

Brush Strokes

Accented Edges · Angled Strokes · Crosshatch

Dark Strokes · Ink Outlines · Spatter

Sprayed Strokes · Sumi-e

↑ Go to *Filter > Brush Strokes > Sprayed Strokes*. Here you can experiment by applying any of the Brush Strokes filters to the mask and adjusting the settings to fine-tune the effect.

↑ Here we've applied the Sprayed Strokes filter to the mask and used sufficiently large Stroke Length and Spray Radius to make the effect apparent in the mask. Click OK.

↑ You'll now have a new layer containing the filtered border. You can now experiment with blending mode options, Hue/ Saturation, and Levels commands— in fact anything you can think of.

↑ Press the Edit in Quick Mode Mask button again to get the standard Marching Ants selection outline. You could now fill this with a color of your choice by going to *Edit > Fill*. Alternatively go to *Layer > New > Layer via Cut*.

→ Here we've set the Border layer's Blending Mode to Difference and reduced the opacity. Flatten the image (*Layer > Flatten Image*) for outputting.

Glossary

Adjustment layer Adjustment layers give you the ability to make non-destructive tonal or color changes to underlying image layers.

Alpha channel An Alpha Channel is a special channel in addition to the standard Red, Green, and Blue channels, which stores information relating to pixel transparency.

Anti-alias Anti-aliasing is a method of smoothing the edges of selections in Photoshop to avoid "jaggies" along the edges of copied and pasted image elements. You'll see an Anti-alias option for most of the selection tools in Photoshop.

Auto Levels The Auto Levels command automatically adjusts the black-and-white points in an image, and can be a good quick fix for images that need just a little contrast and brightness adjustment.

Background layer When you open an image from a digital camera, it will initially be displayed in Photoshop as a single Background layer in the Layers palette. The Background layer can be converted to a standard floating layer by double-clicking it in the Layers palette.

Blending modes Blending modes allow you to blend individual layers with the layers below. You select a particular blending mode in the Layers palette. By default, a new layer is always set to Normal mode, the pixels on the layer have no interaction with those on the layer below.

Blur filters The group of Blur filters can be found via the *Filter > Blur* menu entry. They can be used to generally soften an image or a selection. Blur filters can be especially useful for reducing noise within an image or disguising any artifacts in an image where too much JPEG compression has been applied.

Brush tool The Brush tool allows you to paint onto an image. You can select many brush footprints for the tool itself and control the size, blending mode, and opacity of the brush via the Options bar. The brush can also be made to respond to the pressure applied via a pressure sensitive graphics tablet to control size, opacity, and color.

Crop A method of trimming an image to a particular size, using the Crop tool. Cropping an image can also help in terms of composition, cropping out unwanted image elements.

Canvas Size The Canvas Size command adds a chosen amount of extra space around the outside of an image. By default, the size of the available canvas is limited to the actual outer boundaries of the original image. You can choose how much extra canvas to add, and where around the image to add it in the Canvas Size dialog.

Channels A standard RGB image contains three separate color channels, specifically a Red, Green, and Blue channel. Channels can be treated in much the same way as layers, in the respect that you can

make all manner of adjustments to each individual channel.

Clipboard An area of memory where Photoshop stores copied image data. After using the *Edit > Copy* command, Photoshop temporarily stores the copied image data on this virtual clipboard, so that the image data can be used at a later time, for instance by using the *Edit > Paste* command. All image data in this temporary storage area is lost when closing Photoshop, or by using the Purge Clipboard command.

Color picker A color palette where you chose your Foreground and Background colors.

Contiguous Contiguous is an option available with the Magic Wand tool. This indicates that any similarly colored pixels must be touching each other or interconnected before they are selected together with the tool. Unchecking this option indicates that similarly colored pixels should be selected together regardless of whether they are interconnected or not.

Dots Per Inch (dpi) The term used to describe the number of dots of ink laid down by an inkjet printer per inch. You'll often see the Resolution of a printer described as DPI.

Deselect A command available via *Select > Deselect* that literally deselects or cancels the current selection or Marquee.

Dodge tool A tool that harks back to the days of traditional darkroom techniques that can be used to selectively lighten the tones in a particular area of an image.

Desaturate A method of reducing the amount of visible color and increasing the amount of gray in an image.

Eyedropper A tool used to sample colors from an image or from anywhere on the desktop.

Feather A command that softens the edges of a selection by a selectable number of pixels.

Filters Automated effects available via the Filter menu in Photoshop that can be used to apply a vast range of preset automated effects ranging from artistic natural media type effects to distortion, brush stroke, and texture variants. Most filters present a self-contained dialog box from which the variables within the filter can be controlled.

Flatten The Flatten command collapses all visible layers into a single Background layer, enabling the saving of the file to a file type that does not support images containing separate layers, such as JPEG. Once a file has been flattened, the individual layers are no longer accessible.

Fuzziness The Fuzziness slider, available in the Color Range dialog, controls the degree to which colors matching the current Foreground color are selected.

Gamma Gamma describes the brightness of the midtone of a grayscale tonal range. In tonal adjustment commands such as Curves, the midtone point below the histogram is more accurately described as the Gamma slider.

Gaussian blur One of the most commonly used Blur filters for accurate and adjustable blurring on an image or layer.

Grayscale What we generally think of as the black-and-white display within Photoshop. In this mode, an image can contain a maximum of 256 shades of gray.

Hidden tools Tools that are hidden or nested behind other similar tools in the Toolbar. Hidden tools are indicated by a small arrow next to the currently displayed tool, and can be accessed by simply clicking and holding on the displayed tool.

High key A high-key image is one where the majority of image detail is concentrated in the midtone to highlight areas. High-key images are very soft and flattering.

Histogram A map of the distribution of pixels throughout the 256 levels of brightness within a digital image.

Hue A value that determines the actual color we perceive. In essence, the value that makes Red appear as red, and Blue appear as blue. Where two colors are mixed, the hue changes accordingly.

Interpolate To add pixels to increase the size of an image.

Inverse An option available via *Select > Inverse*, where the current selection is reversed; unselected areas become selected and vice versa.

Jitter Available in the Brush Options for controlling the variance and random aspects of a particular brush's dynamics.

JPEG A type of file compression used in the JPEG file format, which reduces the size or weight of the actual file by discarding image data.

Layers Layers are at the heart of Photoshop image-manipulation and can be thought of as separate sheets of acetate stacked on top of the original Background layer.

Marching ants Marching ants is used to describe the dotted, animated outline around a selection.

Opacity Opacity refers to the extent to which an upper layer obscures the contents of the layer below it.

Options bar The area in Photoshop, across the top of the workspace, with the various options for the currently selected tool.

Palette Photoshop uses palettes to contain the essential tools, devices, and components that are used in the image-making process.

Pixel A pixel is the very stuff of digital imaging. Any digital Photoshop image, or digital camera image is made up of millions of pixels, each one carrying specific color and brightness information.

Quick mask An easy and accurate way of creating masks or intricate selections. Quick Mask mode is activated by hitting Q on the keyboard, and the initial red quick mask can be painted on to the image using any of the Photoshop painting or fill tools. On exiting Quick Mask mode, an active selection is generated, reflecting the shape of the painted mask.

Rasterize Converting a Vector image (made up of paths and shapes) into an image that is made up of individual pixels.

Reselect Found via *Select > Reselect*, this command will reselect the previous active selection. This can be useful if a selection was deselected in error.

Resolution Describes the number of pixels within a digital image. More specifically, the number of pixels per linear inch of an image.

Saturation Saturation refers to the vividness of any particular color. Just as desaturation removes color, increasing the saturation value of a color makes it more vivid and increases the purity.

Stacking order Stacking order refers to the way layers are arranged within the Layers palette. Any layer elements at the top of the layer stack will appear to be in front of any elements on lower layers.

Styles Available via *Window > Styles*, these are a collection of preset combined layer styles that can greatly enhance objects in an image, such as Type object or fills.

Transform A number of methods for distorting the contents of a layer, available via the *Edit > Transform* menu. Options include: Scale, Rotate, Skew, Distort, and Apply Perspective.

Transparency Parts of a layer that contain no image data are considered by Photoshop to be completely transparent. Photoshop supports 256 levels of transparency.

Undo Undo allows you to restore an image, or part of an image, to an earlier state.

Unsharp mask One of the Sharpen filters within Photoshop and one of the most flexible and frequently used. The filter itself works by increasing contrast around the perceived edges in an image, giving the impression of increased sharpness.

Virtual memory A percentage of the computer's hard disk that an operating system uses as temporary extra memory space when the available RAM memory is full. In Photoshop parlance, this is otherwise known as a Scratch Disk, the capacity and location of which can be specified in Photoshop's preferences.

Index

A

ACR *see* Adobe Camera Raw
Actual Pixels *66*
Adjust Sharpness *70*
Adjustment Brush *11, 41, 83*
adjustment layers *22–23, 26, 100*
Adobe *102*
    see also Elements; Lightroom; Photoshop
Adobe Camera Raw (ACR) *10, 38, 39,*
    65, 67, 98
All Layers *77*
alpha channel *20*
anchor points *36, 37*
aperture setting *74*
Apple Aperture *10, 38, 40, 134, 137*
Atkins, Anna *112*
atmospheric effects *94, 97, 104, 146*

B

background layers *20, 21, 26, 68, 82, 89,*
    102, 128, 146, 148
backlighting *27*
barrel distortion *54–55*
batch processing *11*
Bicubic Smoother *47*
black point *14, 16, 18, 22, 136*
black and white *62*
    cyanotypes *112–15*
    hand-tinting *126–27*
    high-key portraits *147*
    solarization *116–17*
black-and-white adjustment layer *23, 104–5*
black-and-white conversion
    Channel Mixer *100–101*
    film and filter *102–3*
    Raw *38, 98–99*
Blend Images Together *139*
blending modes *21, 26–27, 69, 89, 92, 93,*
    95, 102, 113, 116, 117, 124, 125, 126,
    128, 144, 146, 153
blown highlights *124, 125*
blur *70, 148*
    Gaussian *70, 71, 80, 81, 93, 149, 152*
    lens *70*

    motion *71*
bokeh *76*
borders *28, 114, 150–53*
bounding boxes *49*
bracketed photos *130, 134*
brightness *16, 17, 18, 28, 29, 41, 104, 111*
Brown, Russell *102*
brush size *25, 30, 34, 63, 82, 86, 93,*
    115, 143
Brush Strokes *152*
Brush tool *86, 93, 115, 126, 143*
buildings *52–53*
burning *62–63*

C

camera shake *70*
Cancel *50*
Canon *38*
Canvas Size *52, 114, 150*
capture sharpening *66*
cataloging *10, 11, 40*
catch lights *85*
Channel menu *96*
Channel Mixer *119*
    black-and-white conversion *100–101*
Channels *20–21*
chroma noise *65*
chromatic aberration *56–57*
Clone Stamp tool *75*
cloning tools *75, 76, 77–78, 80*
clouds *14, 22*
color adjustments *58–59*
Color Balance *87*
color cast *16, 17*
color channels *18, 19, 20–21, 100*
color coordination *86*
color fringing *56–57*
color infrared *128–29*
color noise *65*
Color Picker *95, 113, 120, 126, 140, 150*
Color Range *32, 60, 61*
color saturation *11*
color settings *58*
Colorize *110*

compact cameras *56, 64*
compression *38*
Content-Aware Fill *79*
continuous tone *44*
contrast *16, 17, 18, 19, 29, 38, 41, 101*
    cross-processing *122–25*
converging verticals *52–53*
Corel Paint Shop Pro *10, 13, 18*
CR2 files *38*
creative sharpening *66*
cropping *38, 39, 45, 48–49, 53, 138, 139*
cross-processing *19, 122–25*
CS2 *70*
CS3 *30*
CS5 *79*
Curves *18–19, 26, 116, 117, 122, 124–25,*
    132, 138
cyanotypes *112–15*

D

Daguerreotypes *126*
dark tones *14*
default settings *25, 62, 64, 119*
deghosting *134, 135*
detail *14, 29, 64, 65, 66, 67, 112*
Details Enhancer *136*
dialog boxes *12, 16, 23, 32, 109*
dodging *62–63, 82*
downsizing *46*
drawing tools *12*
drop shadow *21, 141*
Dry Media Brushes *151*
duotones *106–7, 108*
duplicate layers *24, 26, 68, 82, 92, 128,*
    147
dust spots *39, 74–75*
dynamic range *130*

E

Elements *10, 13, 18, 19, 24, 27, 28, 32, 34,*
    38, 40, 48, 70
Elliptical Marquee *28*
Eraser *151*
eraser tools *12*

Index

Acknowledgments

Additional photography by:
Chris George
Adam Juniper
Steve Luck
Frank Gallaugher